Countrywise

by

Raymond Rush

Illustrated by
Gavin Clowes

Published by

CHURNET VALLEY BOOKS

43 Bath Street
Leek
Staffordshire
01538 399033

© Raymond Rush, Gavin Clowes
and Churnet Valley Books
1997

ISBN 1897949 26 X

Contents

Preface

Acknowledgements

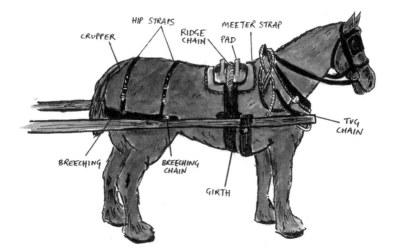

CRUPPER

HIP STRAPS

RIDGE CHAIN

MEETER STRAP

PAD

TUG CHAIN

BREECHING

BREECHING CHAIN

GIRTH

The heavy horse harnessed for shaft work

My faithful Fergy tractor

PREFACE

On an August evening in 1929 a plump little 'Norfolk Dumpling' was born into a farming family - I HAD ARRIVED! My first happy years were spent on this small mixed farm, but times were difficult during the agricultural depression of the inter-war years. My parents decided to sell up and move to a market garden type of holding in Suffolk, where we produced all kinds of fruit and vegetables and had hundreds of free range hens. About ten years later we moved again to a similar, but even more intensive holding, only a mile away. As the income was not sufficient to support me as well, when I left school I became an engineering apprentice in Ipswich.

At the end of my five years training I was called up to serve my two years National Service in the Royal Electrical and Mechanical Engineers and was posted to Shropshire. There I met an attractive young farmer's daughter who didn't wish to become an engineer's wife so following my demobilisation, I changed to become a farmer. After gaining experience on local farms, I worked for my future father-in-law. When he died a few years later, the estate wished to sell the farm. My wife and I couldn't afford to buy it but were very fortunate in gaining the tenancy of this farm in Cheshire where, for more than thirty-five years, we have milked our herd of Golden Guernsey cows twice a day and raised our family.

Many years ago I was asked if I would contribute a monthly article on 'Country Matters' for a new publication - a 'free' newspaper. Although I had only ever written one or two items previously, I did have about ten years' experience broadcasting a weekly country slot on 'Radio Stoke' and had made a considerable number of appearances on television. I accepted the challenge and now, some fourteen years later, my list of subjects to write about are still far from exhausted - even if I am!

So many readers have asked if these articles could be put into book form that, at last, I am doing something about it. But first, just a word or two in explanation. Although each story is self-contained, it often links with others to give a broader view of country life. The original newspaper headlines, put in by the various editors were so good that I have left them in to increase your enjoyment.

The reason for many of the articles having a religious background is that for more than forty years I have been taking services at local churches as a Lay Reader. To help supplement our farming income, I also give talks on a wide variety of interesting and amusing subjects two or three times a week., whilst in my spare time (and I do have just a bit), I enjoy making 'Corn Dollies' and during October each year over nine hundred supplement the fruit, flowers and vegetables in our lovely little ancient church for Harvest Festival.

Acknowledgements

I would like to thank the following for their help over the years :

My loving wife, who has patiently corrected my many mistakes (and not only those made on paper) and tolerated my days of 'withdrawal' whilst writing.

To the past and present Editors of the 'Town and Country Post', Frank and Shirley Dixon, John and Joan Williams, their staff and the printers who have, so far, accepted everything I have written in my laborious longhand, also for their inspired headlines which have summed up the articles and for giving me permission to print them.

The readers of the 'Town and Country Post', who have given me such encouragement to continue.

To Claire, who has managed to make sense of the additions and corrections and has so neatly sorted out the articles on her computer.

It was only a matter of a few months ago, when I was wondering how this book could be illustrated, that I heard of an energetic young teacher, Gavin Clowes, who was wishing to become an illustrator in his 'spare' time. This was in addition to him being very active in all kinds of sports and teaching 'Karate' to the youngsters in the evenings. He has also been very busy modernising his home, has a hard working wife, two lively daughters of a similar age to my grand-children and a younger son. I hope you will enjoy the extra dimension his drawings give to the articles.

1 June 1981 Rabbit Pie
THE CUNNING OF MOTHER RABBIT

There it was, right in the middle of the field - a rabbit
hole. I nearly twisted my ankle in it. My foot dropped
into it when I was only half awake, fetching my cows in
for milking. The early morning mist swirled around,
promising a fine warm day, just as soon as the sun
started to break through.

From experience I knew it was a nesting hole, since
there was only a little freshly scraped soil at the entrance of
a shallow hole. The mother had young and she was at home,
because when she leaves the burrow to feed she fills the entrance hole
to stop predators, such as stoats and weasels, going in after her babies.

When fetching the cows I usually carry a long twitch (a thin whippy stick).
Kneeling down carefully (my arthritis was playing me up a bit - thunder coming,
tomorrow probably), I gently pushed the twitch down the hole. After a couple of feet it
hit something soft, then it pushed on another six inches and stopped. I twizzled the stick
around in my fingers, pulled it out and found exactly what I had expected, fine light
hairs caught on the end, fur hairs from the doe's tummy which she had plucked off to
make her youngsters a fur-lined nest. No doubt about it, she was in there, with five or
six kindlings.

I let them sleep on. In about six months time I can have rabbit pie! Until then I
will let nature take its course; there's room for a few rabbits on my farm after the
devastation of myxomatosis!

But why did the mother nest in a shallow hole in the middle of the field? Well,
she was within a day or two of kindling and the deeper you dig, the harder the soil. She
simply hadn't the time, or the energy, to make a deeper burrow. Had she dug her nesting
site in the hedge bottom, the newborn babies would soon have been discovered, as that
is the predator's highway, but out here in the middle of the field they take a lot of finding
- except first thing in the morning by some fool of a farmer like me, who is half asleep
and not looking where he is going!

Oh, and by the way, my arthritis was right. We did have a very heavy
thunderstorm that night!

GASP! GASP!

2 July Wet Weather Silage
RAINS BRING A HIDDEN PERIL .... FOR THE FISH

My next door neighbours have much larger farms than mine. Their formula for farming is greatly different from my organic holding run on almost ancient lines.

My fields are small, theirs are large. I make hay, or try to if only the sun will shine long enough to dry the grass. Whereas they, like most livestock farmers, have partly removed the frustrations of our unpredictable weather from their system by making silage.

All day and every day, including Sundays, their farmyard clamps have to be filled with newly mown grass. Sometimes the grass is allowed to wilt for a few hours to increase its content of dry material, but this year it hasn't made much difference, since it has been shower, after shower, after shower. The water has been pouring from the floors of their grass-laden trailers as they pass by my farm.

In wet weather the weight of material increases greatly and, under the compression of the tractor and the weight of six to eight feet of wet grass on top, this excess moisture oozes from the silage pit in a form which, in posher circles, is known as 'effluent'.

As this mass of grass warms up, fermentation takes place and the resultant effluent becomes very highly toxic, which means that it is able to absorb vast quantities of oxygen before it neutralises itself. Should any of this waste find its way into a brook, river or stream, it reduces the oxygen content of the water to such an extent that fish suffocate and drown!

In a dry season very little of this dangerous liquid is produced, but this year the handling and disposal of the effluent has been a major problem on my neighbours' farms. It makes me glad I don't make silage, but if this rainy weather continues for much longer, I may soon wish I didn't even have to try to make hay!

3 August Corn Harvesting
PREDATORS FIND EASY PREY IN THE CORNFIELD

How quickly the country scene changes!

Yesterday this twenty-acre field was filled with golden corn. Today it is a bare and empty stubble. The grain, harvested through a gigantic combine, now lies stored in a steel-sided silo several miles away. The straw has been packed into rectangular bales, removed mechanically and stacked unceremoniously in a distant barn, where it awaits the hungry months of winter.

The mechanical scavengers of the straw and grain are followed by nature's carnivores, clearing up the corpses of the slain. Machines work so fast that there is little chance for insects and mammals to escape the cutting, crushing confusion when a world of stems and ears falls into a flattened field around them. No nests remain for the field mice, no fauna for the frogs, no hiding place amongst the short stubble for the humble bumble-bees in their mortgaged mouse holes. All are now easy prey for the predators, the hawk, crow and magpie by day, the owl, fox and badger by night.

How different from the scene of our forefathers. Then it would have taken twenty men to scythe those twenty acres in a day, their wives tying the loose stalks into sheaves and their children standing them in 'stooks', arranged in sixes, eights or tens in the form of an 'A' to let the sun and wind dry them.

By tradition, the church bells had to ring over the stooks for three Sundays before they were considered mature enough to be carted home to the farmstead. There they were skilfully stacked and, if outside, thatched to shed the winter's storms.

On wintry weekdays gangs of men threshed the sheaves with flails in the same sequence that they rang the changes on the church bells on Sundays, which is how bell-ringing began and why the old barns of yesteryear were called the 'Cathedrals of the Countryside'.

In my short farming span I've taken part in the whole cycle of the changeover. From scything the headlands of the cornfield, preparing a path for the first round of 'the binder', to conveying the combined corn to the dockside mills at Liverpool.

But I reckon that as well as giving the insects and mammals more time to escape, the older, slower methods of the past also had their compensations in companionship and friendship among country folk, ways that have long since disappeared from far too many villages. Life was harder, but it was often more rewarding. Most people gained a great deal more satisfaction from their work than they ever do today, with all its hustle and bustle - and, after all, what do we do with all the time which we save?

Yes indeed, how quickly the country scene has changed!

4 September
TREE HOUSE FELL VICTIM TO KILLER BUG

It was already leaning at a crazy angle when I came to this farm, well over twenty years ago. The lower branches of the elm tree were almost touching the ground but, being within reaching distance of my young cattle, they were soon devoid of leaves!

It had stood in this drunken stupor between the five bar gate and the river for very many years. The ivy was inches thick and enveloped the trunk. It reached almost to the tips of the branches and made the tree look as though if it was wearing a green shroud. One of the drooping branches had to be cut off so I could get into the field with my tractor. I remember standing on the tractor seat and sawing as high as I could reach to give me plenty of clearance underneath, but over the years the amputated limb slowly sank nearer and nearer the soil that raised it until the weight of the mighty monster rested on the sawn stump, just as an athlete might rest on his elbow.

It was a tree of character, for on the upper side of its sloping trunk, rooted in the rotting compost of its leaves, which had become trapped amongst the twisted ivy, grew a miscellany of flora - rose bay willow herb and dandelions, whose seeds had drifted in on the air currents, a small hawthorn bush, probably started from a seed eaten by a blackbird or thrush, several varieties of grasses, mosses and a lovely fern, all flourishing together.

The bark on the underside was worn smooth and shiny by my yearling heifer calves. They used it as an itching post to rid themselves of their thick winter coat when the warmer wafts of spring caused the brown branches to graduate to hues of green.

At the end of May the bees murmured around its blossom, which later ripened into little rounded seeds on transparent discs. They also sought the honeydew exuded by the greenfly that sipped its sap in the early summer.

Because of its size, its gentle slope and footholds of ivy, it was an easy tree to climb. My children built themselves a 'tree house' in the uppermost branches. There they passed the long sunny summer days reading, cooking with a primus stove or using it as a fortress when they played soldiers, and, for a fast escape, a rope was dangled to the meadow beneath.

Birds of all kinds used it for nesting, tits in the tiny holes in the trunk, sparrows and starlings in the larger ones. Thrushes, blackbirds and more sparrows utilised the convolutions of the ivy. Woodpigeons and doves built their platforms in the higher branches to raise their 'pigeon pairs'.

It provided shade and shelter for all and sundry, and myriads of insects lived in the ivy. Sun scorched or storm tossed, the tree had its purpose in life - but now it is no more. For like so many of its companions it was struck with the dreaded 'Dutch Elm' disease. The bug which carried the deadly fungus burrowed beneath the bark and infected the tree. The sap could no longer reach the extremities in sufficient quantities so the green hue of spring growth turned yellow, the foliage shrivelled and fell prematurely, leaving behind the skeleton of the elm tree swathed in its ivy shroud.

A pile of ash marks the funeral pyre of the smaller branches. The trunk has gone for coffin boards and the thicker branches have warmed us from the chill of winter for a full season.

No more will the blackbird and thrush wake me with their dawn chorus from its highest branches in the springtime, nor shall I again be able to enjoy watching the treecreepers pluck the spiders from the crevices in its bark. But animals and birds are very adaptable. My cattle now seek shelter under a nearby holly bush and a silver birch sapling has become their new rubbing post.

The starlings have found a nesting site under the eaves of the church roof and the tits have enlarged a decaying hole in the apple tree by the cowshed. The pigeons are nesting in the lofty branches of the Scotch pines, and the blackbird and thrush use the barren twigs at the top of the pear tree for their territorial tattoo, which is even nearer my bedroom window!

As for the tree house - well, my children have long since outgrown such indulgences but, in time, I am sure they will tell their offspring of the marvellous times they had in their tree house when they were young.

As I was sawing up the remnants, I noticed there were some unusual artistic shapes where the ivy had twisted several times around a rotten bough, which I put to one side and later gave to an expert flower arranger. She took them in hand, trimmed and bleached them. They now form the background to some of her outstanding floral displays and everyone asks where did she get those wonderful shapes? Which leads me on to suppose that the moral of this story is that everything in life has a purpose to perform and a tale to tell. The trouble is that, all too often, we abuse the purpose and forget to tell the tale, don't we?

So, if you have anything of interest in mind, why not jot it down. One day your notes may become a book - mine have!

5   October Blackberry Fool?
HOW A FARMER SOLVED HIS PRICKLY PROBLEMS

About this time of year, when I'm taking my cows along the road, a lot of folk pull up in their cars and ask, "Where's the best place to pick blackberries around here?"

I usually send them onto a bit of waste ground a mile or so away, where they won't do much harm. Because it's very rare that anyone bothers to say "please" or "thank you" or even "may I have permission to go into the field to pick blackberries?" and anyhow, if having cared for them season by season, I told them that the best ones were down the village by the old bridle path, I should never have any good ones to pick when I fancied a blackberry pie or my wife wanted to make some jam to sell at the Women's Institute would I?

But did you realise that those brambles haven't always got into the hedgerows by accident. In the days before barbed wire became cheap enough for fencing, the easiest way to confine stock was to grow hedges.

The best stock-proof hedge is hawthorn, but over the years other varieties of bushes creep in and smother the hedge. Occasionally part of the hedge is killed by late frosts, caterpillars or cows horning their heads in the hedgebank soil and exposing the roots. If the bushes die you end up with a hole in the hedge through which the stock will wander.

One of the quickest ways to fill those gaps is to plant a rooted blackberry. Within its first year it will fill the space and send long, prickly stock-proof stems to intertwine with the hedge on either side. It also has the added attraction of producing flowers in summer to provide honey for the bees, fruit in the autumn for pies and preserves, tea from the dried leaves, yellow dye from the roots, navy blue and indigo dye from the berries, or a black dye if the berries are boiled with ivy leaves!

Long strands of bramble will trail along the hedgerow for ten yards or more until, curling downwards they become entwined with the long grasses along the hedge bank. Wherever the stem tips touch the damp soil, white roots will quickly form and a new plant will grow. This extends the looping, leap-frogging action away from the parent plant.

It was these newly formed roots from the outer headlands of the field that were dug up, separated from the parent plant by severing the stem, and replanted to fill the hedge gaps during any month that had an 'R' in it. So blackberries were transplanted anytime from September to April.

In the hope that it would cure their ailments, young children, crippled with disease were passed back and forth through these bramble archways whilst reciting the Lord's Prayer. Animals were also passed or driven through the loops to protect them from evil influences. If bramble stems were plaited in threes (Father, Son and Holy Ghost), they acted as a defence against demons. They were even more potent if plaited into a circle, when they symbolised the crown of thorns.

In the 18th century, when the dead were buried outside in the churchyard instead of inside the Church as previously, the fresh earth mound was protected from witches, evil spirits, the devil and the parson's pigs, by brambles, plaited and pegged into patterns, covering the bare soil. This was also said to have the additional advantage of confining the corpse and stopping the soul from sauntering away!

The prickly stems had other uses too. Long lengths were pulled through a hollow cow's horn, from tip to root, to remove the thorns. These fibrous stalks, split if too thick, were used long before string to hold thatch down, or to stitch straw-rope into baskets, skeps, bee hives, mats and mattresses. They would also make circular targets for the village archers to practice their 'artillery' from the churchyard every Sunday after divine services.

Rabbits have always loved to burrow under the safe canopy of blackberry bushes and many birds build their nests in them, the thorns give an added protection. And, don't make a mountain out of a mole hill, for if you push a few long bramble stems along mole runs, it may well deter the 'gentleman in the velvet waistcoat' from digging up your lawn!

Taking it all round, blackberries have been, and still are, a very useful item in the life of the countryside.

Apart from ourselves; wasps, flies, butterflies, mice and foxes all like the fruit but there is just one word of warning. Raw blackberries should never be eaten after September 29th, St. Michael's Day (Michaelmas). Why? Well folklore (and Revelations, Chapter 12 verses 7-9) say that when St. Michael threw the devil out of

heaven he landed in a blackberry bush and swore revenge. Every year since then he has avenged himself, by piddling on all the blackberries on St. Michael's day - so do be warned and take heed.

Incidentally, that latest car load I sent up the road just called to say that they couldn't find many blackberries there. I got out of that one quite easily. I said it was because it was such a good place that someone else must have beaten them to it and they will have to try a bit earlier next year

That's how I got rid of another prickly problem.

6 November
IT'S THE SURVIVAL OF THE FATTEST

I don't know about you, but at our house we could never remember which way to alter our clocks. We didn't know whether to give ourselves an hour more or an hour less in bed, until we came across the saying, 'Spring forward, Fall back'. Fall is an old English word meaning Autumn, an abbreviation of Leaf-fall.

My wife usually says that when you change the clocks, you change the weather, and this year is no exception to the rule. In Celtic times November 1st not only heralded the winter, it was also the first day of the New Year and was celebrated by feasting, fun and frolics, which had a much deeper significance than many might at first imagine. Let me try to explain, in my usual roundabout way. I'm often asked "Why don't the birds leave the acorns and berries until the bad weather?". Well the answer is quite straight forward really. If the berries were left on the bushes they would wither and wrinkle and become just skin and pip, having very little feeding value, so the birds make full use of the rapidly decreasing hours of daylight by eating as much as possible while it is still succulent. This food turns into layers of body fat they can live on when the fields are frozen and no fresh food is available.

In a similar way, Nature in her wisdom supplies an extra growth of grass at the end of the season. We farmers call it the 'Autumn flush'. It helps to bring sheep and deer into good condition for mating and provides surplus rations for all grazing animals; they convert it into fat, to help keep out the cold in the coming months.

In years gone by, gaggles of geese grazed the gleanings from the corn stubbles. Pigeons, rooks, squirrels and mice ate the acorns. Pigs were allowed 'Pannage' in the woods to rummage around the roots for fallen beechmast, nuts and acorns; all to make them fat.

And we were no exception to that rule! Michaelmas (September 29th) was celebrated with roast goose. All kinds of meats and fruits were gorged with delight at the 'Harvest Home' or 'Horkey Feast', held to celebrate the completion of the corn harvest.

At 'All Hallows Eve' (Halloween), we feasted to the full on apples, pears, fruit and nuts, and if nuts were plentiful, lots of boys would be born the following year!

There next followed a week of festivities for the 'Wakes' at 'All Saints'. A special delicacy was 'Frumetty', wheat cooked on the slow hob for hours to soften it, then mixed with milk, sugar, spices, flour, butter and rum and boiled until creamy. Its nickname was 'windy-gut slop', and children weren't allowed in Middlewich, Bunbury and many other churches after eating it!

November 5th had special village dinners as well as bonfires.

By the next feast day, St. Martinmas, November 11th, all animals for eating at the mid-winter solstice should be slaughtered or the meat would not be smoked or cured in time for yet another indulgence at Christmas

All those feasts and festivals meant that most people ate so well in the Autumn that they, like the animals, put on large layers of fat before the onset of winter.

In women the fat was most noticeable around the body-belt, biceps, bosoms and bottoms. So buxom women with large bosoms became fashionable, while large bottoms were later camouflaged with - or enhanced by - the bustle!

Men tended to store their surplus fat in their stomach. Those who worked for the local corporation attended so many free banquets that they extended their 'corporation', the nickname for an enlarged stomach!

'Plumpness' was the rule of yesteryear and if you look a bit closer at the paintings of the great masters, you will see how chubby were the cherubims and how buxom the beauties, when compared with today's beanstalk bathing beauties - and they say it is all in the eye of the beholder! So fixed was the fashion for fatness that a man wouldn't marry a woman if she was at all skinny - for fear that she might not survive the winter!

It is a well known fact that people who are thin feel the cold more than those who are fat. Perhaps that is why nowadays we tend to spend more on central heating than central eating!

SPEAK YOUR WEIGHT

" ONE AT A TIME PLEASE"

Tinned foods and deep freezers have replaced the need to fulfil ourselves at feasts and festivals, but the birds and animals still have to put on those extra layers of fat to see them through the winter.

So don't be too annoyed if your bathroom scales show you have a little more balance than usual. It may turn out in your favour - it will help to see you through the winter.

So, in late Autumn our changing clocks remind us we shall have to 'fall-back' on our reserves, then when the brighter days arrive, we can all 'spring-forward' into the Summer. See you on the other side - if you survive

SPRING FORWARD

FALL BACK

7 December The Christmas Backlog
THE MERRY REIGN OF YULETIDE'S
LORD OF MISRULE

Wood burning stoves have a voracious appetite, as many people discover soon after they install them.

This week I have been busy on my farm, going around the fields collecting all the timber blown down by the Autumn gales. Nowadays I do it the easy way, using my tractor and trailer, but I vividly remember that in my younger days, whenever I went out for a walk with my parents or granny we would come back laden with broken branches for burning and twigs for kindling.

Both Mum and Grandma wore aprons. When gathering fuel, they would hold up the bottom corners of their apron with one hand to make it into a carrying bag, and with the other hand pick up the pieces of wood. Dad would carry the thicker, heavier lengths of branch over his shoulder, or we would drag them home behind us.

On my morning bicycle ride to school, I was always on the look-out for firewood, which I would collect on my return journey, balancing the logs precariously across the handlebars or, if it was a very heavy piece, I rested it on the saddle and pushed my cycle home.

These longer lengths were stacked upright behind the granary, with dozens of other boughs we had accumulated throughout the year. This woodpile was a favourite haunt for rats, and our farm spaniels would spend hours excitedly chasing around when one was in residence.

Most of the large autumn pile had been burned by springtime. It was one of my regular jobs on a Saturday afternoon, cutting wood for the following week. The wobbly sawing horse bore many a saw scar as a result of my daydreaming of more important things. Large logs had to be split into usable sizes with the axe or, if the wood was knotty, I used iron wedges, knocked in with a 'beetle' (a heavy wooden mallet).

Bushel skep after bushel skep I carried into the back kitchen - the back-house or 'bachus' as it was called, where it had to be stacked neatly, ready for burning on the front room grate, the kitchen hob, the oven or the washday copper fire.

When a tree is cut down by hand it will warm you three times over, first when felling with axe and saw, secondly cutting it into logs and, thirdly, by the fireside.

Resinous larch, spruce and pine were always wanted for kindling - to start the fire. These logs had to be reduced to about finger thickness on the chopping block, using the heavy hatchet.

Generally, hard woods, such as oak, ash, beech, hawthorn and holly give out the most heat. Soft woods - those that grow rapidly - are of less calorific value. All, except ash, need to be dry, otherwise much of the useful heat is lost converting the water or sap into steam.

Woods to be wary of are willow, chestnut, larch and pine, for they will spit and fly, throwing sparks and burning holes in fireside carpets and rugs, unless a fine mesh fireguard is used. Poplar gives off an unpleasant acrid smell.

Silver birch burns brightly and attractively, but its resinous smoke clings to the chimney and is difficult to remove. If the soot gets thick enough, it can become a hazard, and cause a chimney fire.

Elm will burn well if seasoned and dry, but if sappy or wet it smoulders "as slow as the churchyard mould" - but its boards do make good coffins!

For a special occasion include a log of orchard wood - apple, pear, cherry or plum - on your fire. Its pleasant perfumed smoke will rapidly permeate the house. Another old dodge is to scorch a piece of their bark or twigs on a hot fire shovel. If those barks aren't available, roasting chestnuts or the smouldering stalks of lavender or juniper will scent the room for hours with their delightful fragrance.

If you only put one log on a fire the coal will burn even quicker than with no log at all. Two are a little better, three logs are the minimum for a wood fire, preferably lying on a mound of their own ashes. Four will burn well, but five will give out a heat that will make you push your chair back!

Compared with yesteryear, fireplaces nowadays are small, almost insignificant affairs. Even so, nearly threequarters of the heat produced goes to waste up the chimney.

As a compensating amount of cold draught has to be drawn in to the room from around the edges of windows and doors, you become roasted on the fireside but chilled to the bone on the backside!

In former days high-backed chairs and settles helped to alleviate this discomfort. People would also sit on three sides of the fire in an enlarged chimney breast, called an 'inglenook'. Its wide flue was hand-swept by children. Many old houses and halls still contain internal brick or stone footholds that these unfortunate young chimney sweeps once had to climb.

Going back even further into history, the fire was placed on a stone hearth in the middle of the room. The smoke would gradually find its own way out through a central hole in the thatch; or through 'wind holes' or 'wind eyes', under the eaves - the forerunner of our modern windows!

Condensation or leaks in the thatch meant that everywhere and everyone under the drips would soon become as black as soot.

By Royal decree, good wood was sometimes reserved for furniture, house building or making ships, then firewood became scarce. In the days of William the Conqueror, only a tree that had been blown down by a gale could be claimed for firewood - by the finder. To discover such a tree was considered extremely lucky and explains both the origin and meaning behind our present day expression of a 'windfall'. On medieval estates, the poor could gather fuel only by 'hook or by crook'. This meant brushwood thin enough to cut with a hook and branches within reach of a crook. Thicker trees and higher boughs belonged to the baronial estates.

Another word that remains in our vocabulary to remind us of ancient custom is 'backlog'. On Christmas Eve a 'Lord of Misrule' was appointed; he presided over the joviality whilst the yule log burned. To make sure that it lasted as long as possible, the yule log - a heavy tree trunk - was secretly soaked in the river before being dragged home to the hall.

Sitting astride it, the 'Lord of Misrule' entered, to start his reign. The great yule log was placed on the fire and became the 'backlog'. Whilst it smoked, smouldered and blazed, merrymaking, feasting, music and games went on in the hall and there was a holiday for everyone.

When eventually the backlog was reduced to ashes, the festivities finished and the 'Lord of Misrule's' reign ended. Then everyone had to return to work to catch up with the 'backlog' - (of jobs).

8 January 1982
A LAYER OF CLOTHES FOR EVERY DAY OF THE WEEK
IN WINTER

The temperature has remained below freezing for the past two days. The skies are dark, drab and grey, possibly heralding another snowfall? My out-wintering heifers stand huddled in the shelter of the high hawthorn hedge, their tails towards the perishing East wind, which blows so lazily that it doesn't bother to go round you, it goes straight through you!

The young stock spot me coming with the laden wheelbarrow and immediately gallop to the gate. They know I've brought their daily rations to supplement the frozen grass.

Three bales of hay and about one hundred and twenty pounds of brewers' grains, between fifteen of them. It will help to satisfy their hunger, keep out the cold and develop their calves, due to be born in April.

Their coats look rough; each hair is standing on end, just like ours do when we get 'goose pimples'. It is Nature's way of keeping both them and us warmer. Here's how: Tiny pockets of air are trapped between the standing hairs and insulate the warm skin from the cold atmosphere. It acts rather like a forest in miniature, where the wind can whistle and howl over the tops of the trees, but can only partially penetrate past the trunks around the perimeter.

As you may well have noticed, on a cold, windy, winter's day, it always feels warmer and calmer if you are surrounded by trees. Animals possess more sense than we realise and that is why my heifers stand in the shelter of the hedge where the trunks and branches reduce the speed of the cold wind, so that it feels warmer. This was one of the reasons our ancestors so often lived in clearings in woods and forests.

When I'm pushing my wheelbarrow along the road, passing motorists, in the comfort of their heated cars, often laughingly remark on the way I'm dressed. They drive on, clad in summery shirt sleeves, their lightweight jackets dangling from a hook by the side window, no overcoat or warm clothing to hand. Will they never learn? I often wonder how long they would survive if they had an accident or got stuck in a snowdrift. They certainly aren't prepared for the Arctic conditions that exist just outside the confines of their cosy cars. They can laugh all they like. As for me, I don't worry what I look like, because I'm lovely and warm, I'm wearing a layer of clothes for every day of the week, vest, shirt, pullover, jacket, mackintosh, milking slop and sacks. Yes sacks, I have one over my shoulders and another tied around my waist, they not only keep me warm in cold weather, but also dry when it's raining.

In wet weather most waterproof garments have two major drawbacks. The first is that they allow the surface moisture to run down on to your legs and your trousers soon become saturated - unless you wear protective leggings. But this emphasises the second problem. The majority of waterproofs don't 'breathe' through the material, so condensation forms on the inside, especially when you are working. You can soon be as wet with your sweat as if you had discarded the waterproofs and worked in the rain. The advantage with sacks is that they are porous - they 'breathe' and absorb surplus moisture from the inside, as well as from the outside.

If the rain is very heavy and my sack becomes soaked, I simply exchange it for a dry one and hang the wet one in the barn, where it will slowly dry, ready for re-using in

a few days time. By folding one bottom corner of the sack inside the other, it can be transformed into a hood to protect my head, as well as my shoulders.

The other, tied around my waist, keeps the lower parts of my body warmer - it acts like a kilt - and also as an apron when I'm doing dirtier jobs around the farm.

Chilblains are seldom troublesome when people wear clogs. The wooden sole insulates the feet from the cold and wet, keeping them much warmer than ordinary boots or shoes. On very cold days I use the same dodge as my grandfather did sixty years ago. I put a layer of hay in the bottom of my wellingtons to keep my feet dry, warm and sweet smelling. I usually change it for a fresh wad when I feed my heifers. They don't seem to mind. No, we don't waste anything in the countryside! But to keep out an icy wind like we have today, there's nothing better than a layer of brown paper under your shirt. Newspaper is a cheaper alternative, but if it gets damp the print may come off and you could end up with yesterday's headlines displayed on an embarrassing part of your anatomy!

Long ago, people covered the cold, damp, stone or earth floors of their castles, churches and cottages with a thick layer of rushes to help them keep warm indoors. Why not straw you ask? - It is simply that when straw gets damp it goes mouldy, gives off spores that make you sneeze and may make you ill, but rushes, which grow in water, are partially impervious (do not soak up moisture), and therefore keep drier and provide better insulation. Rushes will also last about four times longer than straw, they cost nothing and can be harvested at slack times during the farming year, which is why they were such a popular floor covering in the past.

People also spread a deep layer of hay, straw or rushes over their ceiling rafters. It had a similar insulating effect to our present day practice of lagging the loft with polystyrene or glass fibre and, again, it was much cheaper.

Cottages were also kept warmer by having thicker walls and a roof of thatch, an excellent insulating material which would last up to eighty years, when put on properly.

I've noticed recently that when I comb my hair, my 'thatch' is rapidly falling out. I doubt if mine will last for eighty years, so I've been wondering about doing a spot of re-thatching on myself. After all, I wear a straw hat in summer to keep my head cool, why not a "RUSH" hat

in winter to keep my head warm? Now that would give those passing motorists something to laugh about, wouldn't it!

9 February
THRILLS AND SPILLS IN THE COWSHED AND
A PROMISE OF BABY COW PIE

Hallo there, come along in; my word you're up early, does your mummy know you are outside? She does; good. Now you have a look in here, we've got a little bull calf, born about five o'clock this morning, I should think. See, its back and sides have dried out, but underneath its body is still damp, and it is still wet behind the ears!

Oh! pull the door to, it'll help to stop any draughts - that's the last thing a baby calf wants. That's it, pull the sacking down again, it stops the wind whistling in and prevents the water pipes above the door from freezing.

Yes, the calf was born before I got up this morning. What I've done so far is to smear some carbolic oil on its navel, you'd call it your belly button. It's really its umbilical cord where it was attached to its mother. Carbolic oil helps to stop any infection getting into the calf's system. Now, the next thing is to check his mummy, to see that her milk is clean.

Can you pass me that strip cup hanging on the tap? Yes, it's that aluminium ladle with a black disc on top. When I squirt some milk from each of the cow's four teats onto it you can see if there are any lumps, which we call mastitis, and whether it looks the right colour.

Whoa Daisy, steady old girl. She's a bit sore because her udder is crammed full of milk. That's it, steady old girl, can you see - it's smooth, deep yellow and sticky, just as it should be. The cow's milk is clean, no mastitis, the milk runs off this black disc and into the bottom of the cup. Can you swill it out for me under the tap?

Next we have to teach the calf to drink. He has been trying for some while. Oh yes, he can walk within an hour of being born, he was a bit shaky at first, but he's growing steadier now. See where he's trying to get at the milk, much too high up, that's what we call instinct. The little calf's senses tell it that the milk should be high up between its mother's back legs. But because we farmers have domesticated the cow she now supplies about a thousand gallons of milk a year, instead of the two hundred or so gallons her ancestor produced just to rear her calf.

This means that the udder - the bag carrying all that milk - is now five times as big, so it hangs a lot lower. The calf still thinks the milk comes from higher up - its instinct hasn't caught up with progress.

We will help him get his first drink. He should have some milk within six hours of being born, because this first milk - 'colostrum' - contains most of the antibodies against disease that the calf will need to stop him being poorly for the next few days.

He's wandered round the other side of his mummy whilst we've been talking. Can you bring him back? You'll be all right, she won't bunt you. Aha! she's just sniffing you while she eats her hay. She knows you're only there to help. Whoops, pick him up. Whoops a Daisy! No, you're not supposed to fall over as well. What's that, you've fallen into something - on your knee, never mind, don't cry, wipe it off with a wisp of straw, you can wash it off later.

Come on little calf. Now watch what I'm doing. I stand over the calf and put my two fingers in his mouth, then put his mouth near the cow's teat and squirt a little bit of milk in between my two open fingers, onto the calf's tongue. That's it, he's started to suck my fingers. Another squirt. Whoa! hold still, Daisy old girl, you made me miss the calf's mouth. Oh - it squirted on you instead, did it? Never mind, we'll wipe it off later, you're properly in the wars today.

Another squirt while I put the cow's teat in the calf's mouth and while he's sucking, I'll take my fingers out. There we are, success. The calf's sucking away at his mummy. Oops, he's lost it. See, he's bunting his mummy's udder with his head. Now that he knows what milk tastes like, he wants some more! Come on - here's the teat. A bit lower - you've got it. Whoa, Daisy old girl!

Let's stand back a bit and watch. He's sucking away and his tail's wagging; that shows that he's pleased. Now, look carefully, what's the cow doing? She is licking him just below his tail. That's very important in newly born animals, it's a kind of massage to start his bowels working, yes that's right, he's going to the toilet. She's still licking him and see what is happening. He's drinking her milk in at one end and she is cleaning his mess up at the other.

Dirty? No it's not dirty, it's Nature, it's instinct. She has massaged his backside with her tongue and what he is passing is very rich in some of the foods his mummy needs now that she has calved. Essential minerals, I believe, to help keep her well and free from disease. It's natural for her to clean up everything he does, because long, long ago, predators - wolves or wild dogs - would smell the baby calf's mess, follow the scent and catch, and even kill, the little calf. That's why his mummy cleans everything up.

He's had enough milk now. I'll draw some more out into my bucket and give it to his mummy. Why do I give her her own milk to drink ? Because it's very rich and may help to stop her going down with milk fever. What's milk fever? Any more questions and you'll wear your brain out. Well, the effort of calving this little bull has taken lots of energy from the mummy cow, especially from her blood supply, and if she hasn't enough sugar and calcium in her blood it makes her feel queer and she acts as though she's drunk, she may even fall down and go into a coma. So, to try and prevent that happening I am taking a bit of her 'colostrum' milk - about a gallon - and giving it to her to drink.

Can you drink it? No, it would make you sick, it's much too rich. What we will do though is, tomorrow night we will save a bit, mix an egg and some sugar with it and cook it in the oven. What does it taste like? Like a very rich egg custard, we call it

'beastings' or 'baby cow pie'. Would you like some? Righto, remind me tomorrow night to save the 'beastings', and we'll have 'baby cow pie'.

I think you like staying on the farm, don't you? Listen, someone's calling - it must be breakfast time. The little calf has had his, now it's our turn to have ours!

10 March
WHEN FAKE CUCKOO CALLS CAUGHT OUT APRIL FOOLS AND IT WAS A DISASTER IF THE FIRE WENT OUT

"If March comes in like a lion, it will go out like a lamb", says the time-honoured proverb. This year it was heralded in like a lion by roaring winds and sudden sharp storms, which gave rise to a sight that can only be appreciated from a considerable distance.

Looking Northwards, over 'Bills' mothers', sheets of hailstones were falling in wide bands of slowly descending columns. They stood out in light relief against the darker background of the heavy storm clouds. They also looked just like heavenly versions of the sheets that my wife had pegged out on the linen line earlier, which now hang limp and sodden after the passing deluge. I should have fetched them in, but was so absorbed with writing this article, that I didn't realise they were getting wet - until it was too late! I shall have to throw my cap in first, before I dare venture indoors tonight!

Perhaps it has some connection with why our Saxon ancestors called March the Hreth monath - the rough month, the Hlyd monath - the boisterous month and the Lencten monath - the month of lengthening days, from which we get the name of the church's season of LENT.

Although nowadays we think of March as being the third month of the year, it hasn't always been so. For hundreds of years, in fact from 1200 to 1752, New Year's Day was March 25th, 'St. Mary in Lent's Day', 'Our Lady's Day' or, as we now call it 'Lady Day'.

In the countryside we still have a constant reminder of this late start to the year. Rented farms and smallholdings usually change tenancies on March 25th - Lady Day. I moved to this farm twenty-three years ago, on March 25th, and my rent falls due twice each year, at Michaelmas and Lady Day.

The Saxon word that was used to describe 'rent for land' was 'ferm' from which originate our words of farm and farmer. So a farm was originally rented land. In early days, payment of 'rent' was made by the 'farmer', acting as host to the 'LAND-LORD' and his retinue for a certain number of days each year, depending on the size of the 'farm'. Later it was paid in work, by serving the owner for three days of each week, Monday, Wednesday and Friday, between October and August and on two days a week in August and September. Sometimes an additional payment in goods was required, such as a pound of butter each week or ten eggs (half a score), or enough oats to feed two horses and perhaps a dish of fish at Easter, and a goose at Michaelmas. Also, at all times the farmer and his workers must be ready to follow their 'LAND-LORD' into battle.

As the years progressed, farmers worked less frequently for the Lord of the Manor, and spent more time on their own farms. So their rent and taxes were paid in money, instead of work or goods. This early monetry payment was called 'SCOT', anyone excused paying rent and taxes got off 'SCOT-FREE' - an expression we still use today.

Another forgotten word for rent was 'MAIL', when improperly extorted for protection of property by border brigands in the northern counties, it was called 'BLACK-MAIL'. Similarly, the 'VILLEIN' of yesteryear has become the 'VILLAIN' of today!

But back to March 25th as New Year's Day. Anyone who has tried to trace their family history through ancient documents, written before the change to our present Gregorian calendar in 1752, will find that Lady Day crops up yet again. Dates between December 31st and March 25th were left 'stranded' between the preceding and following years. For example, if we were searching for February 18th, 1665 (by our present reckoning) it would be written February 18th, 1664/65. That is after December 31st, 1664, the last day of the old year, but before March 25th, 1665, the first day of the New year!

You may have heard it said that 'A peck of March dust is worth a King's ransom'. The reasoning behind this is that, providing the ploughed soil dries sufficiently for a bit of dust to form, you may safely get onto the land to work it into a tilth, and sow the seeds earlier than usual. Those few additional days extend the growing season sufficiently to give an increased yield at harvest. When all this extra produce is added up throughout the realm, it is enough to pay the ransom for a King to be released from exile - as was Richard the Lion-Heart in 1194.

BLONDEL SINGING OUTSIDE THE CASTLE LOOKING FOR HIS IMPRISONED KING

At the end of the week of celebrations that welcomed in the New Year on March 25th came April 1st - All Fools' Day. Some people suggest that the foolery may have derived from the mockings and scourgings after the trial of Jesus, or from the Roman feast of Cerealia. But in France, on April 1st, it was the custom for boys and girls to go out into the fields and woods to search for and call the cuckoo. As it was such an easy bird to imitate, many children would be 'fooled'. They'd run home, full of excitement, to tell their parents the good news - Spring had arrived -

for they had heard the first cuckoo. In England a country simpleton was called a 'cuckoo'. The controversy still goes on today - 'Dear Editor, I have just heard the first cuckoo - is this a record?'

One of the quaintest customs of the whole year happened at Eastertime. Because of the difficulty in kindling a fire before the invention of matches, fires burned continuously throughout the year. If the fire should ever go out it was considered to foretell misfortune on the household, as well as very poor management on the part of the housewife.

There was one day in the year, however, when they were purposely put out. That was on Easter Saturday - to remind people of Christ lying in his cold tomb. In the late evening, just before midnight, all the parishioners would walk to the service in the village church carrying their unlit lanthorns (lanterns). The church was in darkness. As the bell tolled midnight and rang in Easter Sunday, the priest would kindle a flame on

the altar. It had to be started in the same way as the Need Fires - by friction - as this did not involve the use of metal (and flints) to obtain the spark. Eventually the rapidly rotating stick would cause sufficient heat for the 'coltsfoot' tinder to begin to smoulder. The priest would blow on it and perhaps add a scrap of previously scorched cloth. Hopefully, it should burn into a flame, which would last long enough to light the Paschal candle - the symbol of the Risen Lord - the Light of the World. The congregation then came up to the altar in turn to light their lanterns from the Easter (Paschal/Passover) Candle.

At the end of the service they rejoicingly carried the light home to rekindle their own fires. Until the following Easter, that fire was the symbol of the Risen Lord and the centre of family life. It would warm them, cook for them, and protect them from the many and various evil spirits which always lurked just outside the range of its comforting warmth and light, especially at night. That is why it was such a portent of disaster if your fire went out in olden days.

Well, March came in like a lion, will it go out like a lamb? I wonder if that saying has any connection with Good Friday - God's Friday and the crucifixion of the Lamb of God?

11 April Food for the Worms
HUNGRY MONTH WHEN FARMER WALKS PLANK AND FINDS WORK FOR HIS TINY 'PLOUGHMEN'

Livestock farmers call April the hungriest month of the year. Throughout the length and breadth of the land, seasoned stockmen are warily watching the weather and anxiously checking their scant stocks of silage, hay and straw, which are rapidly dwindling in spite of careful rationing.

In the fields, the early grasses have not yet grown sufficiently to feed the cows full-time. Turn the stock out too soon, and they will eat all the grass in sight, then have nothing left to follow. Turn the stock out too late, and the grass will grow unpalatable before the cows can eat it. But if the cows have to stay inside much longer, it will mean buying expensive fodder from the market, or expensive concentrates from the merchant to feed them.

Even a few days delay can make a big hole in a small pocket. It can easily tilt the balance from a slight profit to a considerable loss. Every farmer will tell you the same story. The less fodder you have, the faster the cows seem to eat it, and if you have to buy it, they go through it like wildfire! This year, I'm lucky, I have half a bay of hay left in the barn. It should be enough to tide me over this difficult period, when the only things that seem to be growing are the sizes of my manure heap and my overdraft. Still they do say 'where there is muck, there's money'. My bank manager doesn't seem to be so sure about the financial side, but I've certainly got a big pile of muck!

Every morning my task is the same. Six or seven barrow loads of manure have to be wheeled from the cowshed, across the road, up the ramp, along the wobbly wooden planks and tipped onto the top of the heap. I'm probably one of the last farmers in the area that daily 'walks the plank'. On most farms nowadays the manure is scraped out by a rubber squeegee on the back of a tractor, and pushed in to a 'lagoon'. Here the sloppy slurry is stored - until the day you drive past in your car. Then - wham - the obnoxious smell suddenly hits you. It reaches right to the bottom of your stomach, as you pass by the 'freshly fertilised' fields.

My manure heap is of the old fashioned variety. Even when it's being spread it smells wholesome and countrified. It is stable, strawy and solid, otherwise I wouldn't be able to push my wheelbarrow over the top of it - I would sink in! That reminds me, I must remember to ring my contractor to come and spread it onto the meadows within the next week or two.

Years ago, all farmyard manure was

stacked and stored in large heaps like mine. On frosty winter days it was carted out by horse and tumbril and tipped into small heaps, five and a half yards apart, chequer-boarding the fields. When it had further decomposed, it was spread evenly over the ground, using short handled 'four-tine' forks. On arable land it was ploughed under to feed the root crop that always followed next in the rotation, but on grassland it was left to weather for a week or two, to allow the nutrients to be washed into the soil. The strawy remnants were then chain harrowed, to break them into even smaller fragments, that would not clog the cutter bar fingers of the hay mowers.

Yet none of this manuring would be of any value if it were not for the myriads of micro-organisms that constantly work away underground to convert it into plant food. Soil scientists say that in every teaspoonful of fertile earth there exist more living organisms than there are people in the world. It is in fact a gigantic food chain, in which each species relies and feeds upon the product of the others. Rather like the old rhyme:

Big fleas have little fleas, upon their backs to bite 'em,
And little fleas have lesser fleas, and so ad in - finitum;
But big fleas themselves in turn, have bigger fleas to go on,
While these again, have bigger still - and bigger still - and so on.

One of the larger earth occupants we all instantly recognise is the worm. Yet how many of us realise how important it is? It has been calculated that on every acre of permanent pasture, there exists twice the weight of worms working below the surface as stock grazing above. As most farmers have a cow to the acre - weighing about half a ton, this means a ton, or more, worms, burrowing, draining, aerating and enriching the land beneath. Over one and a quarter million 'Lilliputian Ploughmen' to the acre!

It's little wonder that the seagulls excitedly follow the plough, when so much food is being exposed for them. But sadly, after ploughing the living population rapidly decreases. Arable land can only support a few worms. The rest die from starvation - shortage of humus - lack of manure. Even if the ground was sown back to grass immediately, it would take up to twenty years to re-establish the deposed population to its former level and rebuild the fertility of the field.

Hence the maxim: To break a pasture - makes a man; To make a pasture - breaks a man. And it's amazing just how hard those worms do work. If I was to collect all the beneficial worm casts from my forty-five acres, they would fill ninety ten-ton lorries every year! No wonder they are called 'Lilliputian Ploughmen'.

So when you see me pushing my barrow across the road, up the ramp and along the wobbly planks, I'm not only cleaning the manure from the cowshed, but also providing food to fill the stomachs of my 'Lilliputian Ploughmen' - my worms. They will break down the manure into plant food, that will produce even more grass, which I can make into hay, to see me through the hungry month of April next year.

At least it gives a whole new insight to the expression 'Grub Up'!

12 May
HOW FARMYARD PONDS ROSE FROM THE GRAVE

When did you last see ducks swimming on a pond? Or play at ducks and drakes by skimming a flat stone across the surface and counting how many times it bounced? Probably some while ago. Yet nearly every parish once had its pond, usually beside the road and next to the village green. It was of great value if any stacks or thatched cottages caught fire.

Criminals and witches were punished by ducking them into it until they confessed or promised to amend their ways. Farmers would water their animals before the daily journey to the grazing grounds on the outlying common fields.

As a result of the Enclosure Acts of the 1700s many farmers had to move from the centre of the village, to occupy new enclosed areas in the remoter outskirts of the parish. One of the main requirements for their livestock was a good supply of water. Wells could provide for the needs of the farmer, his family and his staff, but animals drank so much that it was too laborious to draw for them so pits or ponds had to be made.

Sometimes the pond was a specially constructed hollow, carefully lined with puddled clay. It would catch the overnight condensation and collect the watershed from the surrounding slopes. It was called a Dewpond. There is a good example locally, just inside the main entrance lodge at Capesthorne Hall. It is now used as a stockpond for the fishermen. Others ponds just happened.

Some started as marlholes from which the clay was carted away and spread onto the nearby fields. It increased the fertility and structure of sandy soil, while the empty holes gradually filled with water and became pits - marl pits. Probably the most common pond was formed from a natural hollow, where either a drain or a wet-weather spring surfaced.

The ditch taking away the overflow was dammed, making the water level rise sufficiently to cater for the needs of the farmstead during the drier summer months. The pond soon became the hub, around which the activities of the farm revolved.

From my younger days I vividly remember that, from early morning until late at night, a continuous stream of residents came to refresh themselves from its water. The heavy cart horses snorted as they drank deeply, before going into the stable to be groomed and fed. They ate their breakfast of crushed oats, while the wagoner went home to have his breakfast of porridge oats.

The cows, turned out after morning milking, nosed aside the green slime and sucked great gulps. Then they ambled along the dusty lanes to the cowslip covered pastures, with only the biting of the flies or the swish of my long twitch to harass them.

By one of the many miracles of nature, within a few hours, that dark, murky pond water and the grazed green grass was converted into pure, sweet, cream-coloured milk!

Darting house-martins and swallows skimmed across the feather strewn surface of the pond for insects. They mixed the mud from the water's edge with their saliva to make their nests. The house-martins' nests were tucked under the umbrella of the farmhouse eaves to stop the rain eroding them. The swallows built theirs in the rafters of the cowshed, where they helped to control the number of flies, which cause and spread mastitis. This

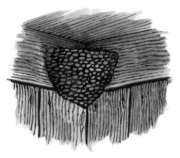

is why swallows are also called the 'farmers' friends'.

Back in the pond, their white tails protruding like miniature icebergs, ducks were dabbling, up tails all, as they searched among the debris on the bottom for extra delicacies. A gaggle of domesticated geese dismembered a female frog that hadn't hopped far enough to get out of reach of their beaks, after adding her contribution to the floating islands of jelly-like frogspawn. Long strips of toadspawn clung to the rushes and waterweeds.

The first tadpoles sunbathed in the warmer water at the edges of the pool. The few that survived gradually grew front legs, back legs, then lost their tails and became amphibians - able to live on land or in the water. But most were eaten long before maturity, by the guzzling geese, the dabbling ducks and the faster fish that occasionally 'plopped' out of the water to catch the dancing gnats, or perhaps by the cackling hens, one of whom proudly announced she had just laid another egg in the almost inaccessible corner of the cartshed.

A few years ago 'tuberculin testing' regulations were enforced and cows were only allowed to drink pure, or 'mains' water. Stagnant pits and ponds had to be fenced off and many quickly became rubbish dumps. The water became putrid and toxic from dumped drums of detergent, steriliser and spray. Life drained away. A covering of earth eventually capped the grave of the farmyard pond. What was formerly the focal point of the farm disappeared.

Heavy horses were replaced by the mechanical horsepower of tractors. Large herds of cows drank treated water from rectangular galvanised troughs in their concrete exercise yards. The house martins no longer built in the shelter of the farmhouse eaves, and the cubicle kennels, which have replaced the collapsing cowshed, contain no swallow nests. And why? Because since the pond was filled in, there was no longer a suitable supply of mud for making their nests.

Ducks that 'dabbled up tails all' are now only to be seen protruding from their polythene packages on the supermarket shelves. The cackling hen lays her eggs on the sloping wire floor of the battery cage and may never see the light of day, let alone peck at a tadpole.

But, in farming - as in fashion - if you wait long enough, the wheel will turn full circle. Many farmers, tiring of the drudgery and monotony of modern intensive systems, have, as a matter or relaxation and conservation, excavated and lined a large hole. Landscaped and filled with water it isn't called a pit or pond, but an ornamental lake! Not to drown their sorrows in, but to clear their conscience! Water lilies, weeping and flowering trees and shrubs have replaced the reeds, rushes, willows, alders and blackberry bushes. Colourful Muscovy ducks swim where there were once White

Aylesbury and Khaki Campbells. Exotic breeds of oriental fowl that were almost extinct now peck at the tadpoles, where previously the Rhode Island Red, the White Leghorn and the Light Sussex ruled the roost.

Instead of working horses, the farmer now has riding ponies, which he hires out for trekking along the local bridleways. They too snort as they quench their thirst at the 'ornamental lake' and the young riders idly skim stones across the surface to see how many times they bounce!

There's nothing new under the sun, or perhaps it is explained even better by Alphonse Karr in a French quotation which, when translated, says "The more it changes, the more it stays the same".

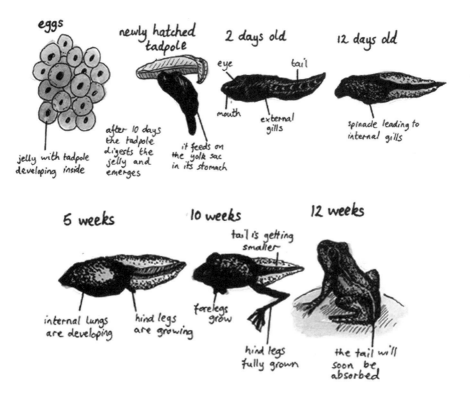

eggs

jelly with tadpole developing inside

newly hatched tadpole

after 10 days the tadpole digests the jelly and emerges

it feeds on the yolk sac in its stomach

2 days old

eye

mouth

tail

external gills

12 days old

spiracle leading to internal gills

5 weeks

internal lungs are developing

hind legs are growing

10 weeks

forelegs grow

tail is getting smaller

hind legs fully grown

12 weeks

the tail will soon be absorbed

13 June Blooming Gardens
AVOIDING A BISHOP'S CURSE

It has been marvellous weather for keeping on top of the weeds. Our garden hasn't looked as neat and tidy for years, and many of the knowledgeable locals are asking, "When's the Bishop coming?" This is a joke of long-standing in our village. It all began, many moons ago, when the only time our garden received any attention was when the Bishop was coming to preach at our church. What's that got to do with tidying your garden, you may ask?

Well, as some of you may know, our garden adjoins the churchyard. Unfortunately, our lovely little black and white church has a very small vestry. Not even large enough for the Vicar and senior choir to robe in comfort. So, on special occasions the churchwardens ask if the Bishop can change into his vestments in the front room of our farmhouse.

In the past, this request has served as a jolly good excuse for my wife to insist that I spend a few days helping her to tidy up the garden and shift the piles of accumulated rubbish. "You can't have the Bishop seeing all that mess. What will he think of us?" she would say. But afterwards I often wondered if he ever noticed, considering the state of some of the parsonage gardens and dilapidated churchyards he must encounter on his journeyings around the diocese.

This year there are several gaps in our garden (nothing to do with the Bishop). The vacancies are caused by the severe frosts of last winter, which took their toll on many older shrubs and plants. Others, such as the roses, were pruned back hard by the searing icy winds. One of our visiting senior citizens told us that her roses had never looked healthier and when we enquired why, she replied "You should always ask your worst enemy to prune your roses. He will cut them back much further than you would ever dare to do. They will think that their days are numbered and will grow away and blossom as you've never seen them bloom before." "But", she added with a twinkle in her eye, "the trouble is that nowadays, I haven't any enemies left, I've outlived them all! This winter Jack Frost has done the job for me and, with my rheumaticky joints, perhaps he is now my worst enemy".

Her explanation about the extra urge to blossom because the roses thought their time was up suddenly jogged my memory. When I was young, every year, Dad used to thrash the trunk and branches of our walnut tree with a heavy chain to bruise the bark. This was supposed to produce more walnuts. Just as in the old saying "A woman, a dog and a walnut tree, the more you beat them, the better they be". I don't have any practical experience of beating women or dogs, but I do know that the tree always produced a bumper crop of walnuts! When my father sold up and moved to another farm, the new owner thought it cruel to injure the walnut tree - and he didn't even harvest a handful, which just goes to show that there's often more truth in those old rhymes of country lore than meets the eye.

Probably the thrashing that the plants, shrubs and trees took from the winter winds is the reason we are now enjoying such a profusion of flowers - they fear their end is near. I'm sure you cannot have missed the beautiful sight of the hawthorn bushes, laden with so much blossom that they looked as if they were carrying a coverlet of snow.

Scores of people have asked us the name of the attractive yellow flowering 'creeper' that covers much of our farmhouse and out-building walls, and has been such a picture this spring. Its official name is 'Kerria Japonica', but most country people call it 'bachelor's buttons'. This is because its small round flowers resemble the buttons which, years ago, had to be taken off garments or they would be shattered between the heavy wringer rollers as they squeezed the water from the

weekly wash. These special bachelor's buttons didn't have to be sewn back on each time. They were fastened by a metal cotter, or ring, on the reverse side of the garment. Eminently suitable for un-domesticated bachelors.

When grown as a shrub in the garden 'Kerria Japonica' will only reach a height of about five feet but, if supported against a wall as ours are, they will tower tall above the gutters, fifteen or twenty feet high and be covered with masses of small bright yellow button flowers, which last from mid-April to late May. I use them as a reliable guide to my farming routine. The cows usually stay outside at night when the first flower buds are bursting and the calves go out to pasture as the flowers are finishing.

This year a blackbird built its nest in one of the climbing bushes on the wall by the front path and all went well until the young hatched. As the chicks grew, the parent birds became increasingly noisy with their alarm calls whenever one of our nine cats appeared around the corner. Eventually the inevitable happened; Thomas our foraging tom-cat, was in no doubt when he went closer to investigate the cause of the commotion. He climbed the creeper and had consumed three of the five fledglings before we could stop him.

For the safety of the remaining pair, my wife confined the cats to their quarters in the straw loft for a week. The last we saw of the two survivors was mother blackbird feeding them in the buttercup covered pasture by the river... but, back to the garden ....

Nowadays, my wife and I try to keep it spick and span, not in case of a casual call by a Bishop, but because it is seen by so many visitors. Almost every week during the summer people come by car and coach to learn about the customs and traditions of our ancient church. They smell the scents of the countryside, admire the surrounding scenery, pace the paths, secretly sample the strawberries, ruminate over the rhubarb, cuddle the kittens, caress the calves, flee from the ferrets, or watch me making 'corn dollies' in my workshop.

Many get bitten by the myriad of midges that seem to prefer ladies who have just had a 'hair-do', or men who have splashed themselves all over with that powerful lure that attracts all females - especially female midges and mosquitoes - but the makers don't mention that in their advert!

In spite of such drawbacks, many say they are coming back next year for a second helping and, as we are also getting a new Bishop installed in September, it probably won't be long before he pays his respects to our parish. When he comes I expect we will be asked if he can change in our front room.

There used to be a widespread belief that if a Bishop didn't like you he would plant his curse upon your garden and up would spring ground elder - still often called by its country name of 'Bishop's Curse', and, as we'd rather receive the Bishop's blessing than any more ground elder, it seems we shall have to keep our garden up to scratch for some time to come.

14 July
FATED FETES

The weather forecast for the weekend said it was going to be dry and bright until Sunday night. I turned my sodden hay all day on Friday but, instead of the clouds lifting and clearing, they were lowering and thickening. Drops of drizzle on Saturday morning did not bode well for our Village Fete.

As with weddings, title fights and many other ceremonies, the preliminaries, parleys and subsequent events are often more exciting than the main function - so it sometimes is with our Fete.

We have an ancient vicarage standing in spacious sloping gardens with a dawdling stream dividing the lawn. For country clergymen of yesteryear, with a good stipend and suitable staff, it was a superior residence, but nowadays our bachelor vicar has to manage it almost on his own, just a bit of help with mowing the lawns by a local lad. So the bulk of the banks, paths and hedges become very overgrown.

One evening at the beginning of the week of the Fete, a team of willing farmers and other helpful parishioners gather to take the equipment out of the outbuildings and lofts, to paint, repair and replace whatever is thought necessary and try to straighten the garden up a bit. Twenty years ago we used to do it with scythes and slashing hooks, then came the era of the motorised mower, overtaken in turn by the rotating, air-cushioned 'flymo'. But the youngsters of today don't believe in getting callouses on their hands using hooks, scythes or even mowers. They prefer to get them elsewhere - sitting in an air-conditioned tractor cab, cutting the grass mechanically behind them. Up the banks and down the dells they skilfully manipulate their monstrous machines. Nowadays there's usually only myself who turns up with a scythe to cut round the awkward corners and under the low boughs where the tractors cannot reach. The grass and brambles look better cut, but if it's going to be a dry week (certainly not this year) it might become a serious fire hazard, so everything is raked up and carted away on a tipping trailer.

We all enjoy the companionship that this working together brings. One year, one of the farmer's sons, raking over a rough area, suddenly disappeared. His distant cries for help emerged from the dark depths below. He had actually discovered the site of the sewage soakaway that the builders had been seeking for years. The heavy tractor had cracked the rotten timbers, which had later given way under his weight. He had to be hose-piped down and went home for a change of clothes. Every year since he has had his leg pulled with such comments as 'mind where you walk', or 'don't step into it again'.

Because of the many empty rooms at the vicarage, boxes, bundles and bags of equipment are scattered all over the house. There was great concern one year; no-one could find the long lengths of bunting that adorn the garden, criss-crossing from the trees to the house. The house and buildings were searched again and again, but to no avail. The vicar was informed and on the morning of the fete we heard that he had found them in a bag in his bathroom! One of the choirboys cheekily suggested that perhaps he hung them up when he took a bath!

Another time a company of Girl Guides were 'in camp' on the Glebe meadow, helping with the preparatory cleaning up. All went smoothly until the day of the Fete, when it was discovered that the vicarage well, overloaded with the demand for the so much extra water in a hot season, had run dry. I received a desperate phone call

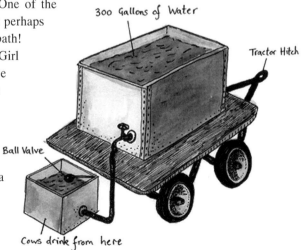

300 Gallons of Water

Tractor Hitch

Ball Valve

Cows drink from here

from the vicar, "Could I help?" In some of my fields the cows drink from a mobile water tank, filled every other day in hot weather, so, denying them the pleasure of quenching their thirst until the fete was over, I filled the 300 gallon tank and took it to the tea rooms. Little did the customers realise that this year not only the milk, but the water as well, was by courtesy of the cows - and we never received a single complaint!

What makes our annual event different from all others is that we have a large mere almost on the doorstep. Our young 'Water-Lily Queen' is rowed across this lake in a boat shaped with hardboard to look like a large swan. On arrival at the vicarage staithe she is crowned by an equally elegant young King. The pageant then processes along the driveway to the sloping gardens, led by a bagpiper in full ceremonial highland dress, or at least that's what should happen if everything goes according to plan, but often it doesn't. On one occasion, a squally cross wind sprang up just as the 'swan' boat was leaving the distant shore. Even the expert boatman, rowing brilliantly, couldn't stop the wind from buffeting the boat towards a sand bank, where some of the stewards had to wade out, waist deep, to release the boat and its royal personage.

Another time someone accidentally flagged the 'swan' to start too early. It sedately crossed the mere long before the King's procession arrived to greet it. The organiser was shouting away furiously 'go back, go back, we're not ready, go back'. But above the laughter, the elderly oarsman either didn't hear or didn't want to - and tied up at the staithe a full five minutes early, much to the amusement of the large crowd and the annoyance of the agitated organiser.

I think it was two years before last when the waters were very choppy, the committee wondered if they ought to cancel the crossing, but decided to carry on as they had organised a safety boat to row behind to pick up survivors! Both boats set off according to schedule, but both soon started to take in water. The 'Queen' had to put her feet up on the seat and sit sideways on, so as not to get her flowing robes wet from the rapidly rising bilges. Then disaster struck. The oarsman, pulling extra hard to combat the cross wind, choppy surface and half-filled boat, snapped one of his oars and the 'Swan' started to waltz around in the wind. Fortunately, such a circumstance had been catered for, there was a spare set of oars in the safety boat which quickly came to the rescue. Unfortunately before it reached the 'Swan', it took on board so much choppy water itself that it, the rescue boat sank, overloaded with water and spectators. What a calamity so far from the shore. Few onlookers realised what had happened. As the flotsam drifted towards the 'Swan' boat, the oarsman grabbed one of the floating oars, and continued rowing towards the staithe. Eventually, yet another boat was dispatched to pick up the 'rescue boat' survivors who were wading in the middle of the mere.

This year the usually dusty driveway was awash with muddy water, where the tenant of the Glebe land had been ferrying his silage trailers home to his farm. He had to go along the very narrow lane that leads past three charming thatched cottages which, alas, are all empty at the moment. Their previous occupants have moved into the old people's bungalows of the area, after giving a lifetime of devotion and service to the village and its activities. These former neat cottage gardens, with the chickens fed mainly on house and garden scraps and a pig fattening in the sty, have suddenly disappeared under a jungle of briars and weeds. But I digress. What I meant to say was that at the entrance to the vicarage gardens, instead of in its usual place because of the mud, was the fortune-teller's caravan. In previous years this was a genuine gypsy caravan, coloured in all its traditional splendour, with a log fire beside the base of the steps and a simmering iron cauldron hanging from its tripod, but this year it was a two-berth car caravan.

The fortune teller's first customer had just settled down when 'bump' - up went the front end of the caravan. 'Someone' had forgotten to lower the stabilising jacks. Both occupants were thrown in a heap at the back. They had to climb to the centre of the caravan to balance the load before it could be righted. There were many suggestions of appropriate predictions that the fortune-teller might have been telling her client at the time - "Your life will be full of ups and downs", "You may be in for a windfall", "Something surprising may happen to you soon", "Don't worry about things that go 'bump' in the night, they'll soon start going bump in the daytime as well"!

Almost every year someone - and not always a child - manages to slip into the stream, sometimes they are walking backwards to take a snapshot, sometimes absent-mindedly, and occasionally jostled by youngsters, while trying to cross over the very narrow brick bridge. There's a splash, and shoes and socks to dry in front of the vicarage fire, or a hurried purchase from the 'next to new' stall to hide the embarrassment of a large round wet patch in a very 'difficult to explain' area.

Another incident happened when one of the choirboys won a bottle of wine on the tombola. He drank the lot, jumped the stream several times successfully before finally falling face down into it. Then he collapsed, out to the world, dead drunk, behind the parish produce stall. As retribution for his sins, he spent the next day being 'dried out' in hospital.

From late afternoon onwards, one of the local ladies runs a hot-dog stall near the vicar's front door. The smell of sizzling sausages and frying onions permeates the surrounding area. Some years it happens that the crowd has already dispersed, left for home early because of a passing shower. It's no use having a lot of bread rolls, sausages and onions left on your hands - that's where the profit is - so, not slow to miss an opportunity, one year it was decided to take everything, lock, stock and barrel, to the clay pigeon shoot just starting half a mile away, on the other side of the mere. All the foodstuffs and equipment were loaded into the Vicar's mini-bus. Off he went, the lady

beside him chatting contentedly away. What neither of them realised was that the through-draught from the open window had enlivened the charcoal fire and started the fat smoking, causing a great black cloud to emerge from the back of the minibus. Courting couples along the lakeside, cuddling in their cars or watching the ducks, pipped their horns in alarm. One or two gave chase amidst the smoke. It wasn't until he pulled up at the shoot that the vicar realised something was burning, other than his ears!

On the Sunday morning after it is all over, we meet yet again to tidy everywhere up and put the equipment back into storage in the outbuildings. Deposited bottles are re-crated for return, the bunting is bundled into bags, boxes of litter picked up and burned beside the boundary wall, where it has been fired for years. Then someone suddenly remembers that the vicarage has just had a central heating system installed and one brick's depth away from our fiery furnace was a five hundred gallon tank of fuel - just the other side of the wall. Why it didn't go up in flames we shall never know - but it caused a bit of excitement at the time, and we've shifted the site of our bonfire since.

This year, however, the rain did manage to keep off. The crowd, although not as large as usual, must have spent more generously, for we finished up with a suitable surplus that will help to keep our ancient church solvent for a further season.

15 August
STAY ON THE 'SAFE' SIDE IF LIGHTNING STRIKES

I was sure it had struck something nearby. Luckily the electric lights didn't go out completely, they flickered and then came back on.

Whenever I see the lightning flash, I automatically start to count. Every five seconds before I hear the rumble of thunder means that the storm is a mile away, but this time I didn't even have time to start counting. The flash and the crash came together, so the storm must have been right overhead. Last time I heard such a bang was when it struck an oak tree in the churchyard, 100 yards away.

When lightning strikes a tree, the current passes downwards through the sap until it reaches the earth. As each flash contains about five hundred million volts, it

immediately transforms the sap into steam, with such explosive energy that it blasts the bark away from the trunk. Trees that survive this ordeal usually remain scarred for life, with a strip of bark missing from the topmost branch to ground level. Fortunately for the trees, static electricity takes the path of least resistance. Sometimes, if it has been raining hard before the lightning strikes, the high voltage will travel down the outside of the wet bark instead, causing only a dark burn mark which disappears with time.

Many years ago, a neighbour had several beef cattle killed. They were sheltering under a hedge when the lightning struck an oak tree, to which was stapled the barbed wire fence. The current flashed along the wire and killed them instantly. Each one had a singe mark down its leg, showing where the energy had travelled to earth.

Our ancestors recognised the fact that oaks were struck more often than any other tree. They dedicated the oak to Thor, the God of Thunder, and used to hold many of their religious ceremonies under the 'Broad Oak'. They also had the mistaken belief that lightning would never strike twice in the same place. Pieces of wood from a struck tree were hung in the rafters to prevent their houses falling victim in the future. Acorns from that tree also provided immunity. Curiously enough, when Victorians introduced window blinds, at the end of the pull-cord was an acorn emblem - to stop the house being struck by lightning!

The long, iron tie-bars that stopped house walls from bulging were also thought to lessen the risk of damage by lightning. If they ended with an 'X' on the outside wall, they invoked the help of Christ.

An 'S' represented a snake or a serpent, which was itself thought to be the product of lightning. As the forked flashing tongue of the snake was like the forked flash of the lightning, it was believed that lightning would never strike at its own kind. Even today, adder skins are sometimes found hanging

from the rafters of old cottages, whilst added protection was afforded from houseleeks, which were encouraged to grow on the roofs.

Elderberry, rowan and ash trees planted near the house would help to ward off witches, who could 'whistle up the wind' and cause a storm!

One of the few places where you were thought to be safe was sheltering under a hawthorn or holly tree. These were both 'holy' trees for amongst their roots and branches lived fairies who would protect you from danger. The hedges of the great droving roads that once spanned our countryside were marked, at intervals, with holly trees. They had the dual advantage that the drovers could follow the track in all weathers and were able to seek a 'safe' shelter if caught in a sudden storm.

In the 9th Century, all churches had to place the effigy of a cockerel on top of their steeple by order of a 'Papal Bull'. These decrees, issued frequently by the Pope, were designed to keep Christians alert and disciplined. But if they were issued too frequently they became just another 'load of bull' (Papal bull). The original intention of the cockerel was as a warning to everyone to be on their guard against the devil, and not to

deny Christ - as St. Peter had done three times before the cock crowed twice. But it was soon discovered that if the effigy worked loose, the cockerel's large tail acted as a rudder, and kept the head pointing into the wind. So it was allowed to swivel, to indicate the direction of the wind and it became a weather-vane or, as we call it now, a weathercock.

I was also told of an entirely different reason recently, when an elderly lady pointed out to me that "They put the cockerel on top of the steeple because if they had put the hen up there instead, it would have been too far to go to fetch the eggs!" - but that might develop into a Cock and Bull story! Nevertheless, the cockerel remains as the symbol of St. Peter.

Storms were feared in olden days, especially at harvest time, as they would damage and flatten the corn, making it difficult to reap and ripen, so hardship or famine could follow. As a deterrent, when a storm was gathering, the parishioners would ring the church bells to try to deviate its path away from the village. Another religious connection with storms is the lectern which holds the bible in Church. Jesus nicknamed two of his disciples, James and John, 'Boanerges' - the sons of thunder. In many churches the lectern is a carved or cast eagle - the thunder bird, the symbol of St. John the thunderer! and the symbol of the word of God in the 'Revelation' - a flash of lightning! And have you ever noticed that the head of the eagle often points to the right - the north side of the church? This is because, by tradition, heathens stood on the North-side, the devil's side, and the converted Christians on the South side - God's side. When I was young I had to sit on the South side for an entirely different reason - so that the Vicar could keep an eye on me - for at that age I often behaved like a little devil!

I can also remember that at the first rumblings of thunder my granny would go around the house and cover all the mirrors. Then she would put all the scissors, knives and other metal objects away out of sight and, lastly, when the storm drew near, close the curtains and pull down the blinds to stop the lightning being attracted to the house. In thundery weather my dad used to put the milk churns in a tank of water, with a wet sack over them, to keep them cool. Publicans laid iron bars over their beer barrels to stop the contents from souring. Any damage done was said to be by 'divine judgement' and even today lightning is classed, in insurance terms, as an 'Act of God'.

But this time it didn't strike the church or churchyard, it hit an oak tree at the bottom of my neighbour's garden. It blasted the topmost boughs and half the trunk to smithereens. Some large heavy pieces lie on their farm lawn, thirty yards away, and smaller pieces are scattered up to fifty yards distance.

Although I don't believe in a lot of these old superstitions, I think I'll put a piece in my loft - just to be on the safe side!

16 September
THE HARVEST, SAVED FROM THE FLAMES

If anyone had told me at the start of the haymaking season that I would still be working in it at the beginning of September, I would never have believed them, but it has happened.

There is an old country saying that any fool can make good hay in good weather. What it doesn't mention is what you do with the stuff when it is constantly raining! Most farmers nowadays conserve the grass by making silage, but even that needs the crop to be gathered dry for the best results.

As I remarked in an earlier article, my small acreage doesn't lend itself to 'modern methods', so I continue to make hay. But why so late in the season? There are several reasons, all culminating in the last field to be cut. Earlier in the year my daughter named her wedding day at the beginning of July. As I didn't fancy working away in the hay fields and missing the preparations for her great event, I decided not to cut any grass until after the occasion. To make sure that the grass didn't grow too forward, go to seed and lose its goodness, I grazed the young stock on the hay fields, letting them eat the spring flush of grass. They grazed the last field well into June before I transferred them to the banky pastures by the church, which are too difficult and dangerous to mow.

The wedding arrangements went far smoother than I imagined, and I was a proud father - leading my daughter up the garden path - to the church! It was a brilliant day - just right for haymaking, but the grass wasn't ready, so I didn't worry about it and, anyhow, there were more important things to hand. The constant stream of relations and friends who had brought gaily wrapped parcels before the wedding, returned after the event, and during the following week, to view the presents. It was well into July before the furniture and gifts were transferred to their new home, and I could settle down to farming again.

The small outlying fields were cut first, followed by a large field a week later and, almost immediately, two more small meadows. In spite of occasional showers, dreary days when the clouds didn't break until tea-time and a wheel bearing that disintegrated whilst working, the fields were cleared within a fortnight. All the hay was dry and sweet-smelling. There's nothing to this hay-making - it's child's play. Only six acres left to cut, it will soon be finished, or so I thought.

SWATH TURNING

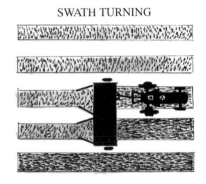

The grass in this last meadow wasn't quite fully grown, so I spent a couple of days straightening the garden. The cow pastures had thistle stalks and bogs of grass which looked unsightly. I had them topped and spent a week, in between showers, baling a couple of loads of 'thistle hay'. At last the fields looked tidy. Only that six acres left to harvest - easy! It was only early August when the contractor arrived to mow the grass but the very next day the weather broke.

TEDDING

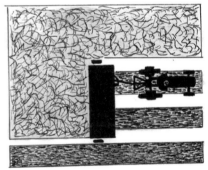

Showers interspersed with rain, day, after day, after day. A dry spell was forecast and my hopes rose, I would turn the hay - that would make it rain - and it did. Eight times that hay was turned, and eight times it rained. It was the last week in August and my wife and I had planned to have a short break. My younger son was also due for a week's holiday, so instead of milking a large herd on a big farm, he milked my small herd on my little farm - a cowman's holiday. "Don't worry about the hay Dad," he said optimistically, "I'll get it in for you while you're away". Well, to give him his due, he did try, very hard. Every fine moment he spent spreading it out, turning it over and rowing it up. Then, just as it was ready to bale, down came the rain, not once but twice during the week.

Ironically, we were touring the eastern counties, and on several occasions could count up to ten-hundred-acre fields of straw all burning at once. What a waste it seemed to a stock farmer, burning all that valuable feed. But beside the fields were row upon row of rotting round straw-bales from previous years, which told their story. The cost of transporting them to where they were needed was more than they were worth. It was more economical for the farmers to burn the straw where it lay and direct drill the new corn into the burnt stubble than plough and sow by traditional methods. The stench of the smoke infiltrated everywhere. The only place we found the smell welcome, was when it masked the mustiness of some of the seldom used churches that we visited!

ROWING UP

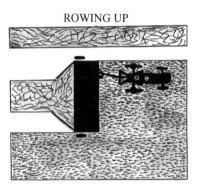

It rained on the day of our return. My son met us, dejected - the hay was still out. More heavy rain fell on the cold Bank Holiday Monday and I imagined the hay would be black, mouldy and riddled with fungus. When it dried I would have to be like those East Anglian farmers and burn it to get rid of it. On Wednesday morning it rained, but became bright and breezy in the afternoon. I went across to turn the hay and, to my amazement, found that it wasn't black, it wasn't even mouldy, it was still worth salvaging. I set to work with renewed vigour, tedding it with my machine, that lifts it off the ground, tears it apart, then scatters it behind for the sun and wind to evaporate the moisture. It was reshaken every two hours, for that is how long it took to cover the field. I had to leave it to give a lecture, fifty miles away, in the evening, but next morning I was back at work in it early.

The forecasters said four days of fine weather; I wasn't so sure, they've been wrong before. That afternoon I put the now rapidly drying hay into recognisable rows, five feet apart. Friday morning I went round the rows and fluffed them up with the tedder and the rowing bars, to let the wind circulate freely through the swaths. Then home to the telephone to book the baler for the late afternoon - he couldn't come! The baler was six miles away baling straw, enough work till Sunday, could I try to get someone else? I went back to the field to continue working the hay, whilst my wife phoned around the local farmers. "Sorry - we're baling our straw", said the first. "Sorry, we're combining, baling, carting, we're up to our necks in work," said the second. "We haven't got one," said the third, "else you could borrow it with pleasure".

The next farmer we tried was silage making. Then we struck lucky, we found a baler who could come, but not at five o'clock as he had another job to do then, he'd come about three o'clock. In fact, about half past two his machine was compressing the now tinder dry hay into manageable rectangular bales. By four-thirty only the outside swath remained. We usually leave that row until last as it takes the most drying, being so near the hedges and trees. We had been so busy working in the hay, we hadn't noticed the storm clouds coming over the horizon, until they blotted out the sun.

BALING

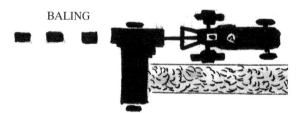

It started to spit with rain. I tore round the field, throwing the bales away from the path of the tractor on that last round. We finished! It was raining steadily. I uncoupled the hay turner and hitched up to the trailer, just as the first of my helpers arrived. Then came my neighbour's son with another tractor and trailer to help cart the bales into the barn. I carried on with the milking. Soon after six my other son and my new son-in-law joined in and we were a very happy gang working merrily away together.

The rain gradually died out. It wasn't wet enough to spoil the bales, but it had temporarily stopped another baler that was half way through my neighbour's crop. We completed our carrying soon after seven o'clock, unloaded the trailers, and had a drink. Then we all went to my neighbour's field to get his in. He wasn't expecting our help and was standing the bales up on end, so that any further rain would run off them. We carted and stacked, carted and stacked, until all his was safe too. One load had to stay

in the fields overnight as I hadn't any lights on my tractor to take it along the road to his farm. We had finished my neighbour's hay, as well as my own. One of my bales had broken, so I fed it to the cows next morning. They munched away at it contentedly - and I had thought, more than once, that I should have to burn it!

At least when Harvest Festival time comes round, I shall be able to sing "All is safely gathered in" - even if it was September when I finally gathered it!

17 October Halloween
HOW THE BESOM BECAME A WITCH'S BROOMSTICKAND WHY WE STAND WITH OUR BACKS TO THE FIRE!

Have you ever seen a witch riding across the star-studded sky on her broomstick? Have you ever lit a candle and put it inside a turnip lantern at Hallowe'en? Or, like me, warmed your backside by a bonfire, while watching the fireworks on Guy Fawkes night, and wondered what was behind it all? I will try to unravel the origins behind some of these past beliefs and put them into present day perspective.

How did the besom broom turn into a witch's supposed method of transportation? Some softwood trees suffer from an affliction made by a bug which burrows under the bark and causes an irritation. As the tree cannot scratch itself, like we can, it grows extra layers of bark to cover the area. These cankerous thickenings continue to grow all through the summer, and form a cluster of distorted stems and leaves. Our ancestors called them 'Witches' brooms'. They said that witches used them, under cover of darkness, to journey quickly from one place to another. These malformations often occur on silver birch trees, the branches of which are used to make besom brooms, which were found in almost every household in bygone days, hence the modern caricature of the witch riding through the sky at night, astride her 'besom' broom!

But why hollow out a turnip face and light it up on October 31st? In Celtic days, long before the Roman calendar was introduced into this country, the first of November was not only regarded as the beginning of Winter, but also the first day of the New Year. It was thought that all the spirits of the departed returned to re-inhabit the earth for two days of freedom. Food and drink were put ready to welcome them, and a candle lit to guide them home. So that they would know which candle was acting as a homing beacon for them, it was placed inside their own skull. It would also help to scare away any evil or unwanted spirits. Of course, nowadays, we don't use an actual skull. Instead, we fashion a face from a hollowed mangelwurzel, pumpkin, turnip or swede, to look grotesque, and so deter witches and evil spirits. For the rest of the year, those real skulls used to be fastened on the projections of their primitive houses, for decoration and to guard their homes by warding off unwelcome visitors.

This same idea was later adopted by the free-(stone)masons when they built

churches. Hideous grotesques and gargoyles were carved on the outside of the church to frighten away evil spirits and deter bad thoughts so that only good ones might enter the building and enjoy the company of the carved cherubims inside!

What is the meaning of Hallowe'en? The feast of All Hallows is better known nowadays as All Saints Day - November 1st. It began because, so deep-rooted was the influence of superstition and the fear of the supernatural in olden days, that when Christianity gradually replaced former religions in these northern latitudes, this season continued to be associated with the return of the dead. The saying "If you can't beat them, join them" must have been known even then. For, in 835 A.D. the church authorities responded by changing the feast of All Hallows from May 13th to November 1st. The previous day, October 31st therefore became 'All Hallows' Eve or, as we call it today, 'Hallowe'en'.

But the traditions of the past continued, unabated, under the guise of the new name. Not to be beaten, in 968 A.D., the church retaliated by making November 2nd the Feast of 'All Souls'. Christianity now also had two days of recognition of the spirits of the departed. Yet still the new religious ideas made little impact on the habits of the heathen. From about 1200 A.D. nobility and the ecclesiastical hierarchy were allowed to be buried within the sanctuary of the church, upon payment of a suitable fee, called Lairstall or Pit money. It was soon realised that this was an easy source of income. The religious authorities therefore let it be known that the more money you gave to the church in your lifetime, or in your will when you died, the nearer the altar you could be buried and the better your chances would be of going to heaven. The less you gave, the further from the altar you were buried, as is well explained in the epitaph from Kingsbridge, Devon, which reads:

> Here lie I at the church's door,
> Here lie I because I'm poor,
> The further in - the more you pay,
> Yet here lie I - as warm as they!

Those with no money at all were buried outside in the churchyard, often in communal graves, and as another epitaph exclaims:

> Where they went to, and how they fares,
> Nobody knows, and nobody cares!

So, from about 1300 A.D. and onwards for the next four hundred years, it became the fashion for the wealthy to be buried, by their relatives, in shallow graves inside the church.

That is why, when you go around old churches, you will usually find the Lord and Lady of the Manor, or the Esquire and his wife, are entombed at the East end or have a special side chapel all to themselves. They believed they were buying their way into heaven. But a problem soon arose. As wealth increased, more and more people were buying burial plots in the church. How could the Church authorities continue burying for rich rewards, when the floor of the church was finally filled? Which is where previous beliefs came back into their own. At the West end of the nave, generally, was dug and lined an underground vault called a crypt, ossuary, bone house or charnel house. Periodically the corpses of those who had been buried the longest were dug up and their bodies and bones stored in the charnel house. In this way fresh burial sites were instantly made available for sale.

But the charnel house would soon have become full to overflowing if it hadn't been for reintroducing yet another custom. People said that when the spirits of the dead were set free to return to earth at midnight on October 31st, not all came from serving their various Gods above. Many, many more, came from torment in the underworld or, as it was later called, purgatory or Hell.

To release these poor unfortunates and save their souls from everlasting damnation, it was theologically thought that, providing their mortal remains were burned, their spirits could rise with the heat of the flames into paradise and be saved. To accomplish this, on All Hallows Eve, the parishioners would build a large fire in the churchyard. Onto this fire were carried all the bones from the charnel house. Because the bones were put onto the fire it was called a BONE-FIRE or, as we say today, a bonfire!

But you're probably thinking "We don't have a bonfire on October 31st, we have ours on November 5th". The reason for the change was that in 1605 a group of Catholic conspirators planned to blow up the Protestant King and members of his Parliament. They were thwarted, Guy Fawkes was caught in the cellars and for his part in the plot was hanged for treason, not burned as many people think.

The following year, in an order which provoked anti-Catholic fervour and curried favour for his own cause, King James I decreed that, in future, November 5th was to be a public holiday and special 'Thanksgiving Services' were to be held in all churches (this continued until 1859). Bells were to be rung, and the bone-fires transferred from October 31st to November 5th.

> Remember, remember the fifth of November,
> Gunpowder, treason and plot.
> I see no reason why gunpowder treason
> Should ever be forgot.

The fireworks that we enjoy are simply modern versions of the ancient symbols of noise, fire and light that were first used by the Chinese to drive away demons associated with the underworld.

The reason that I stand warming my backside by the bonfire while watching them, goes back even further. According to folk-lore, when the Ark was riding out the deluge, it sprang a leak. A dog put its nose in the hole to stop the flow, but the hole grew bigger. The animals informed Noah, who, in his wisdom, sat upon the problem - and solved it.

As offspring often inherit the characteristics of their ancestors, that is why, even today, a dog's nose always feels cold, and a man stands with his backside to the fire - warming it!

18 November
ENJOY YOURSELF ON NATURE'S CAROUSEL

During the past few weeks Nature has treated us to another marvellous free show of her spectacular annual performance. The changing colours of the countryside....

Against a general backcloth of autumnal tints, have been highlighted a range of hues, from the deep, warm coppery bronze of beech leaves, through the brown lustre of the oaks, to the yellow streaks and splashes on the leaves of the silver birch. Now, their function finished, the fallen leaves lie, dank and darkened, mouldering in fungus infected heaps, where they have been whirled by the wind or removed by rivulets of rain along paths, pavements, or galvanised gutters, to rest in a bedraggled mass, blocking downspouts, drains and ditches.

The reasonably mild weather has meant that my cows continue to go out both by day and night to forage the remnants of the autumn flush of grass. They also feast on fallen acorns. Two of them ate too many and started to scour but this was soon remedied by giving them a wad of hay during each milking.

Rooks have been relentlessly quarrelling over their territorial claims in the branches of the oak tree, cawing and warring with one another, until they have filled their crops to capacity with forty to fifty acorns. Then they fly on to the adjoining pastures, carrying further acorns in their beaks, bury them under the turf, and fly back for more. They are so intelligent that during the winter they will return and dig up those acorns for a meal - providing that a foraging fieldmouse hasn't found them first!

I have heard countryfolk say that if you plant more acorns nearby, the rooks will only dig out the ones which they have 'planted' and will not tamper with the rest. Rooks 'planting' acorns in this way may explain why we farmers often find a young oak tree growing in the middle of a field and wonder how it came to be there. In all probability the bird that stored it either died before he could retrieve it - or simply forgot it!

The short length of oak stem and the cup which holds the acorn in place, look just like a pipe. In my earliest days at school we used to collect them to have a 'make believe smoke'. Later we learned to hollow an acorn, make a small hole near the bottom, push in a straw or hollow stem, fill the bowl with dried 'monkey tobacco' (wormwood - artemisia), light up - and smoke it behind the bicycle shed at school. As we grew older our horizons widened, and acorns were used as ammunition in our home-made catapults. My uncle showed me how to make my first one. It only needed a forked hazel stick, a shaped length of rubber cut from an old car inner tube and two pieces of string to bind the rubber into the split ends of the crutch. Within half an hour I could send an acorn whizzing after the sparrows that perched on the ridge of the school roof. What I did not realise was that the headmaster was walking by on the other side. Half an hour later my catapult was resting beside its many compatriots in his study 'confiscation locker' and I had great difficulty sitting at my desk, having received six of his best in recognition of my achievements!

I enjoyed making acorn 'pop' guns too. The barrel was a nine inch length of

elderberry branch, its pith burned out by a red hot poker, heated in the living room fire at night. The plunger was a good length of hazel stick that would just slide inside. To use it, an acorn (peeled if too large) was banged into one end of the barrel with the plunger stick, another acorn similarly plugged the other end. To fire, the plunger was held firmly between my stomach and the end of the barrel, the barrel was grasped with both hands and pulled quickly towards my tummy, aiming it roughly as I did so. The stick pushed the nearer acorn along the barrel, the sudden increase of air pressure forced the further acorn to 'pop' out and travel some twenty or thirty yards towards its target. The gun was reloaded by ramming another acorn into the nearer end. I used a small piece of board to protect my tummy, which would otherwise get quite sore after a few plunges. I also tried to use that piece of board, unsuccessfully as it happened, to shield another part of my anatomy after the headmaster had somehow again managed to get in the way of one of my projectiles!

It's years since I saw a youngster with a 'pop' gun, yet in my childhood they were all the rage. Perhaps it is because their parents no longer have a fire to heat the poker to bore the barrel!

One of my jobs when I was a lad was to collect bushel baskets of acorns to feed the pigs. Nowadays they fall to fatten the pigeons, partridges, pheasants, rooks - or my cows. Whilst, overhead, skeins of Canada geese fly further afield, like shaftless arrowheads in their 'V' formations. They are going to glean the uncultivated stubbles, eat the sprouting winter corn, or slither and slide across the messy machine mauled potato patches where damaged and discarded ones lay on or near the surface. Like other birds and animals they are eating extra food to convert into layers of fat, to help them survive the severity of winter.

Deciduous trees do just the opposite, they become dormant. Their limbs, once clothed with an energy consuming camouflage of leaves, now stand stark, like naked skeletons, shrouded only by an enveloping pall of fog. Yet the reason for the downfall of the old leaves, is the new buds that are already forming beneath the bark. In a few months time they will be transformed into mature leaves themselves.

So the cycle of the seasons continues on its ceaseless carousel, round and round, for ever and ever, and we are the lucky spectators of Nature's ever changing scenic roundabout.

19 December Christmas Customs
THE PIGS THAT WAXED FAT ON PLUM PUDDING

By tradition, Christmas preparations begin with the mixing of the pudding on 'Stir-up Sunday', as the collect for the Sunday before Advent relates. In olden days this pudding was a meat broth, breadcrumbs and dried fruits - 'porridge' - under a crust of pastry. It contained prunes, which are dried plums, hence its name - Plum pudding, though now we make it stiffer and use currants, raisins and sultanas, instead of dried plums. Everyone in the family had a stir for good luck. It had to be stirred three times clockwise (not widdershins), while three wishes were being made, though only one would eventually be granted.

The mixture was put into white earthenware basins, covered with a layer of greaseproof paper, pleated to allow for expansion, and held in place with a linen cloth, also pleated and firmly tied around the flanged rim of the basin. The puddings were boiled for several hours in saucepans of water, on the kitchen hob before being put into the pantry to mature. They were boiled again before eating.

In my courting days, I worked for my future father-in-law. To cut down on the condensation in the kitchen, we used to boil the dozen or so puddings for four or five hours in the wash house copper outside. It made life a lot easier, except for the time when one of the strings came undone, the cover came off and a large basinful of pudding disintegrated into the boiling water. But in the countryside nothing is ever wasted. What was initially a disaster for us, meant extra nourishment for the pigs. They guzzled the gooey mixture down in great gulps when it was added to their swill over the next few days. They became so sleek that they rewarded us by gaining the top prize, and the top price, at our local Christmas fatstock auction. They had eaten part of our Christmas dinner and, in their turn, became part of someone else's!

On Christmas Eve a sheaf of corn was always hung in the branches of the apple tree for the garden birds to feast upon. It was an ancient belief that at midnight all cattle tied up in the warmth of their byres (cowsheds), knelt in their stalls in homage to the birth of the baby Jesus - providing no-one was watching. The next day each animal was given an extra sheaf of oats.

Corn was harvested about three weeks earlier than it is today. This gave the straw a much higher feeding value, the complete sheaf being fed to ruminants, thus saving the time and expense of threshing and milling. Oats for horses, on the other hand, had to be crushed or ground before being fed, otherwise the grain would pass through their stomach undigested. Robins and sparrows would follow horses, hoping for a hot breakfast from any oat seeds passed out in the dung!

A bit of stolen hay fed on Christmas day brought luck to the stable and byre - but not if you were caught taking it from your neighbour's farm. To avert evil a four leaf clover was hidden in the hay lofts above the cattle.

In many places Christmas Day is let in by 'first footing', as the New Year is in other parts. This is a carry over from the Anglo-Saxon period when December 25th was also the first day of the New Year. As soon as possible after midnight the 'first foot' to cross your threshold should be a handsome dark haired young man carrying a hunk of bread, a lump of coal and some salt, often in a chamber pot. This denoted that during the year you would have sufficient food, warmth and money (salary from salt) - what the chamber pot was for is anyone's guess!

Woe betide you if the 'first footer' should enter left foot first, be auburn haired, cross eyed, lame or flat footed, as these were all symbols of bad luck. While anyone with eyebrows that met in the middle meant that a death might follow, possibly by hanging.

Frumetty was a favourite dish at all festivals - wheat boiled in water to swell it then boiled in milk with spices and honey added. It was a great delicacy and some was always put in a dish outside for the fairies. It's nickname was 'windy gut slop'.

Should you need to venture to the bottom of the garden on Christmas morning - to visit the apiary - you might well hear the bees humming the 100th Psalm 'Make a joyful noise unto the Lord', but which chant they use is difficult to say.

Most farmers milk early on Christmas morning. The tanker drivers usually arrive an hour or so before their normal schedule so that they too can finish and get home to their families in time for dinner. But the milkman won't be calling for mine this Christmas. By then I shall have finished for the season! Every year a cow needs about a couple of months rest before she calves again and produces a further ten months supply of milk. Since my cows all calve in springtime, I don't find it economical to feed extra milk producing concentrates at this time of the year. Most of my cows are drying off and the small amount of milk they are giving hardly covers the bottom of the bulk tank. By Christmas it probably won't warrant the Milk Marketing Board calling to collect it. The few cows that are still giving a drop will only be milked once a day, to supply us in the house. At last, I may be able to have a lie-in on Christmas morning, for about the first time in thirty years of farming!

20 January 1983
WHEN THE RATS RAN RIOT IN CHURCH

I noticed the first signs of their presence this morning, when I turned my cows out. There, lying on the stackyard path, beside the dutch-barn were some wheat ears, each having about two inches of stem. Only one group of pilferers chews them off at that length, then carts them away so carelessly that half are lost on the journey - and that's RATS.

The rats had obviously discovered my store of wheat sheaves stacked on top of the hay bales. Each year, from late autumn onwards, my farm is liable to an invasion by them. They only have to travel a few hundred yards across the fields from the picturesque lakeside at Redesmere.

It happens like this: During the summer, townspeople by the hundred come with their children to feed the ducks and swans, coots and grebes. What these daytime visitors don't realise is that in good weather more food is offered to the birds than they can eat. The surplus gets washed to the edges of the lake. Late at night, after the courting couples have finished their kissing and cuddling and left for home, out come hordes of rats to feast on the waterlogged food. In the autumn, as the days shorten and become colder, fewer people come to cast their bread upon the waters and the waterfowl population, expanded by migrating flocks, can now cope with all the food that is given them and very little finds its way to the shore for the rats.

As the lakeside food supply diminishes, the rats forage further and further afield, until finally they emigrate to the local cottages, houses or farms where food and shelter is more readily available. This is the important time to try to catch them; whilst they are still hungry and searching for a future foodstore. Then they will accept the bait I have put down for them and, hopefully, soon die. But once they become acquainted with their new surroundings they are much more choosey in their eating habits. At this stage they also start to seek out a safe nesting site, to protect them from their domesticated predators - the cat and the dog.

Usually it is in some almost inaccessible place, such as inside a cavity wall, behind the barge-boards, along the roof eaves; under the floor; in the thatch; behind the insulating panels of hen-houses, cow byres and piggeries; or, in my case, in the warmth of the hay bales. There is no end to their cunning and craftiness in selecting a suitable haunt.

Although I regularly renew my rat bait, some fight shy of proffered food and prefer to find their own. These are the rats that can become a menace, for when they breed they teach their offspring to survive by avoiding the poisoned bait as well. Wherever you keep stock, be they cattle or sheep, pigs or poultry, they have to be fed, and that food has to be stored, often for several weeks before it is used. That's where the rats come in - through holes, nibbled and gnawed over-night in cracks, crevices and corners of doors and floors, by rodents who have grown long in the tooth during the soft season of summer. Once they have gained a foothold on the farm no woodwork is safe from their attention, unless it is clad in a protective armour plating of tin or steel.

In my earlier farming days, corn was delivered in hessian sacks, which would contain one to one and a half cwt, according to the density of the contents. Nowadays my feeding stuffs arrive wrapped in twenty-five kilogram plastic or paper sacks, but it makes no difference. The rats rip and claw at the bags with teeth and feet and strew the contents on to the floor, contaminating it with their tell-tale elongated dark droppings.

As they waste far more food than they eat, and are such repulsive and pestilent creatures, they have always been ruthlessly hunted. Nearly every countryman has his own particular memories of past encounters with this furry fiend, which he reels off whenever he has a captive audience, and I'm no exception to that rule. Many years ago they caused quite a commotion at the top of my garden.

At first sight there may not seem to be much of a connection between my poultry pen and the ancient half timbered church that stands only a few yards away, but rats once provided the missing link. These particular ones had gained a foothold under the floorboards of the fowl-house. I had noticed a few fresh holes, but never imagined there might be more than the odd rat about. Having a bout of enthusiasm and a bit of spare time one day, I nailed some syrup tin lids over the holes in the floor and dug in a strip of fine mesh wire netting all around the outside of the pen to deny them access. My troubles disappeared.......

It was some six weeks or so later, the congregation sat silent in church. I had conducted the first part of the evening service, the vicar had taken over and was half-way through his sermon, when suddenly the church erupted. All hell seemed to break loose. Shrieks and screeches, scuffles and scamperings, squeaks and squeals came echoing from under the floorboards and moved rapidly about beneath the pews of the petrified parishioners. The commotion slowly subsided, the sermon and the service ended abruptly. The churchwardens hurriedly held an extraordinary meeting of the Parochial Church Council, who decided to investigate the matter further.

On walking round the outside of the church they discovered that the iron underfloor ventilation grids had almost completely rusted away. The well-worn tracks that ran from them to a nearby grave and the scattered droppings that littered the area, left them in no doubt that, since being banished from my poultry pen, the colony of rats had sought sanctuary in the church. However, the congregation weren't willing to put up with all that noise during future sermons, something had to be done. A vote was taken and it was decided to poison the rats. The Vicar jokingly exclaimed afterwards, that had the voting gone the opposite way, they might have decided to keep the rats and get rid of him!

Although poisoning sounded straightforward in theory, it proved rather more of a problem in practice. The rats took the bait in gradually diminishing quantities, showing that they were dying off but, by the following Sunday, the church was being infiltrated with an unusual aroma. A few days later the stench was almost unbearable. There was no mistaking the origin of the odour, the corpses were decomposing.

A couple of carpenters were called in. They had to remove the majority of the floorboards to get at the many sources of the smell and I eventually buried nearly a bucketful of carcases. Unfortunately, the rats had also excavated large quantities of soil in the creation of their labyrinths. They had thrown this damp soil against the floor joists where traces of both wet and dry rot were discovered. All the infected timbers had to be treated at considerable expense.

The soil was levelled and the floorboards replaced. Some

were screwed down instead of being nailed to make future inspection easier. The rusty ventilator grids were renewed with an earthenware variety that should remain vermin proof indefinitely. The smell diminished and the church services returned to normal.

So if you ever join our congregation and you happen to see the faint flicker of a smile cross my face during the sermon, it may well be that something has reminded me of the bedlam that arose on the night when the refugee rats from Redesmere ran riot in the Church.

21 February
TWILIGHT FANTASY AS JACK FROST 'PUTS IT TOGETHER' AGAIN AND COWS CHANGE INTO FIERY DRAGONS

"It's really 'putting it together' this morning". That's a countryman's way of saying that it's freezing very hard. My hands are tingling as I push my wheelbarrow load of hay bales down the road to feed the out-wintering heifers on the further fields. The heavy shower of wet snow, which fell before the gale finally blew itself out last night, has frozen onto the windward side of gates, fencing posts and trees, and given them an ethereal appearance. While in the crisp stillness of the early air, the dark oily smoke from the blacksmith's newly-lit forge drifts lazily downwards. It rolls across his snow flecked garden, filters through the hawthorn hedge, then hangs as heavily as a morning mist in the holes and hollows of the adjoining field.

On the permanent pasture opposite, a flock of seagulls, driven inland by yesterday's tempestuous storms, search vigorously for food. They are joined by hordes of rooks, jackdaws and starlings who chatter noisily among themselves as they lever the frozen cow pats over with their beaks, then greedily gobble the grubs and worms that have taken refuge beneath.

So far my journey has been downhill, but it is a lot harder pushing the loaded barrow up the next incline and I have to 'put my back into it' to keep it moving. The heifers are waiting expectantly at the gate for me. Each of the hay bales splits into about ten wads, which I spread into a large circle. I always make sure that there are more piles of food on offer than animals to eat them. I do this deliberately so that even the shyest feeders among them needn't go hungry. If any are hiked away from one pile by an aggressive superior, they can walk to the next vacant heap of hay and continue feeding.

I count them carefully to check that none has broken out, wandered away - or been rustled in the night! I then cast an experienced eye over them to see that they are in good condition. Eyes bright, ears erect and - the surest symbol of good health - wavy lick marks which cover their coat in a criss-crossing pattern that shines like silk in the speckled sunlight and shadows cast by the latticed branches of the silver birch trees above. Yes, all are present and correct.

I arrive home with my empty barrow just in time to witness another common country occurrence. The blackcurrant bushes suddenly burst into a chorus of song as crowds of sparrows fly in from all directions. Chirping excitedly, and hopping from branch to branch, they gather for what I believe is the courting custom of one of their companions. A couple of minutes or so later the ceremony is completed, the commotion ceases, the spectators disperse and the garden returns to its silence. The flustered female, the object of their attentions, ruffles her feathers, gives a little shake, the feathers replace themselves, sleek and smooth, into perfect position. Then off she flies to join her mate and seek a suitable site for their nest.

Only a few yards away the free-range chickens slither and slide down the ice-covered exit board from their fowl pen slip-hole. Their feathers fluffed against the cold, they huddle together in a frost free corner of the run. Some stand stork-like on one leg whilst warming the other under their feathers. Around them straddle and strut the cockerels. They sense that with the lengthening days, Spring will soon arrive. Occasionally they fight one another for dominance in the peck order of the flock. After each skirmish the victor mounts the highest point and crows in triumph to let the whole world know that he has won, and is often answered, or challenged, by another cockerel on the next farm.

By late morning the sun, still shining from a cloudless sky, has gathered enough strength to melt the snow on the cowshed roofs. As the water drips from the downspouts into the cooler shadows of the cowyard it freezes into long tapered icicles. About midday the cows go out to exercise and browse. Some go straight to the water-trough, where they have to break the thick layer of ice before they can drink, long and deep from the cold draught.

Looking to the east, the view of the distant Pennine hills is so clear that against the backcloth of a light covering of snow it is quite easy to distinguish the dark stone walled outlines of field and farm boundaries fifteen miles or more away.

The snow has thawed from the flat surfaces of my fields and exposed the close cropped green grass, but the shaded indentations of former furrows and drains still contain a covering of snow. From this green and white mosaic can clearly be seen the east-west cultivation characteristics of countless centuries.

The enlarged sun was just sinking below the horizon when I walked across to fetch the cows back inside. The grass crunched crisply underfoot and the keenness of the frost was biting into my skin. But the cows weren't bothered by the cold conditions. Some were still foraging the frozen grass, others lying down, were contentedly chewing the cud. Each cow ruminated on the regurgitated grass for about forty seconds, then she swallowed. The lump disappeared down her throat, there was a pause for a couple of seconds, then a fresh lump travelled from the rumen - the cow's first stomach - up the throat and into her mouth. Each batch of partially digested herbage was masticated (munched) about forty times. That's why cows are called ruminants. I call them anything but, since they are in no hurry to move!

They slowly raise their front end onto their knees, lift their rear end up completely in one continuous movement of their back legs and, lastly, finish straightening their front legs. Next as they are not being unduly harassed they S - T - R - E - T - C - H . Then they arch their back and go to the toilet. Most animals do the same, as soon as they are disturbed, nature calls. The cows slowly amble towards the gate, leaving in their wake a trail of steaming manure heaps looking like miniature volcanic eruptions. As they walk they snort the water vapour from their warm lungs into the cold air. It momentarily turns into a mist which, in the fantasy of twilight, makes them look like a herd of ancient dragons, belching forth fire and smoke, to terrorise all except St.George and me. After milking they stay in the warmth of the cowshed overnight.

11 pm I feed them another wad of hay, the windows are thickly glazed with icy ferns. Yes, Jack Frost is certainly 'putting it together' again tonight.

22 March Spring Sowing
A TROUSERLESS FARMER IS ALL SET TO SOW HIS WILD OATS

On these first fine days of Spring there emerges from every field and furrow the deep throated expensively thirsty, roar of tractors. Farmers are busy trying to catch up with a backlog of ploughing which in previous centuries would have been completed several months ago.

Cultivations continue with modern technological machines which cost the earth. They are expected, by some miraculous means, to transform the sticky soil into a suitable seedbed, a job that in past generations was done free of charge by Jack Frost and his flurry of snow maidens. Today we think we farm efficiently if we have a tractor to every fifty acres of ground. Yet before the recent era of horsepower, either of machine or beast, it was large bodied cows and bullocks who ploughed and tilled the arable fields of our country.

These oxen were hardy animals. The cows produced a calf annually and gave milk to drink or make into butter or cheese. They worked the fields and at the end of their day provided stewing steak for the farmer and his men. They were so economically bred that they lived entirely on straw in the winter and rough grazing in the summer. You compare that with the fuel a tractor consumes today!

Each team of eight oxen was capable of maintaining a 'hide' or 'carucate' of land - eighty acres of heavy clay or one hundred and twenty acres of sandy soil. This size of farm was considered sufficient to sustain the farmer, his family and his staff. The oxen were housed four abreast at one end of the four-bay farmhouse, the family lived at the other end. Each helped to keep the other warm. That is why so many old farmhouse rooms are sixteen feet wide - the width of four ox stalls - one bay.

But, coming back to the arable fields, it was the unwritten law of the countryside that all heavy land should be ploughed before Christmas. Then the frosts and snows of winter would break the clods of clay into a fine and even tilth ready for the spring cultivations. At some time during the month of March, or as soon afterwards as possible, the surface of the soil would dry sufficiently to produce a sprinkling of dust. At this stage the farmer would take a yoke of oxen (two) into the field to prepare it for sowing.

His implements were often as economical as his oxen. To make a harrow to level the furrows, he would lift the gate off its hinges, and lay it flat on the field. From the adjoining overgrown hedgerow he cut several prickly branches of holly and hawthorn. These he interwove between the five bars of the gate and so made a 'do-it-yourself' bush or gate harrow at no cost - I have used one of these myself and they are very effective. After tying a long twisted rope of straw to the head and heel ends of the gate, the harrow was harnessed to the oxen. Not, as people fondly imagine, by attaching the ropes to their yokes, but often by tying the ropes to their tails. Unfortunately, as they dragged the harrow across the field, there were occasional boulders or tree stumps projecting above the surface. If the harrow caught against one of these it would come to an abrupt stop. But the placid oxen didn't, they kept walking sublimely on.

It was, therefore, not unusual in the countryside, to come across oxen with shortened tails, or in some cases, no tails at all. However, if you were working your oxen and you happened to have the misfortune of pulling its tail out, at least you knew what you would have for dinner next night, OX TAIL SOUP! The practice of tying implements to the tails of oxen was banned by an Act of Parliament in 1734.

As the gate harrow levelled the field in strips, any sizeable clay clods that remained unbroken were jumped upon, to break them down to a manageable size. It was because he hopped from one clod to another when preparing the seedbed that the countryman received his reputation of being a 'CLODHOPPER'. Levelling completed, the next job was to sow the corn. Before the introduction of the corn drill in 1740 by Jethro Tull, the seed was broadcast. Handfuls were scattered in a semi-circular arc in front of the sower. He carried the seed corn in a halved sack, or a specially shaped metal container called a 'seed-lip' which hung just above waist height from straps slung around his shoulders. Each handful had to be thrown in rhythm with his walking, or it would be difficult for him to keep his balance and scatter the seed evenly. If the broadcast corn were left on the surface it would be exposed to the elements and become food for the birds.

So it was necessary to harrow the field again after sowing, in order to bury the seed beneath a protective covering of soil. But, inevitably, some seed remained on the surface. It was a tempting bait for the many rooks, pigeons and other birds that flocked to the surrounding trees. They eagerly awaited an opportunity to fly down and feast on the germinating grain. To scare them away the farmer employed young children to run around the fields from dawn to dusk, beating a tin drum or rattling clappers. If they slowed their pace and reduced their din, the farmer would shout and tell them to increase their noise and 'run like the clappers'.

A major breakthrough in corn growing came when it was discovered that the seeds would germinate better if they were planted in shallow holes. To achieve this the farm-worker was provided with two three-feet long knob-ended dibbling sticks. Shuffling backwards across the field, he pressed them alternately into the soil, leaving two rows of holes. His wife and older children would follow, dropping four seeds into every hole. "One for the rook, one for the crow, one to rot, and one to grow". The field was harrowed again as before and the children 'set on' crow scaring at one penny a day.

The farmer noticed that if the ground was warm when the corn was sown it would germinate within three or four days and be out of danger from the birds. But, if the soil was cold, it might take two or three weeks for the green blade to appear and he would have to pay out many extra pennies to the young bird scarers.

He therefore tried to devise some simple and reasonably foolproof system of testing the temperature of the soil to ensure that it was warm enough to sow his grain and save his money. He eventually solved the problem by getting down to fundamentals. Walking out into the middle of the field, he removed his trousers and sat on the bare soil. If he felt uncomfortable he would delay his sowing and save his pennies, but, if the soil felt warm and pleasant it was time to sow his seed.

So if you are ever passing my farm and you happen to see someone sitting in the middle of the field without his trousers on - it's probably me - testing the temperature of the soil, just to be on the safe side, before sowing my WILD OATS!

23 April Spring Cleaning
WHEN FATHER PAPERED THE PARLOUR AND THE SIDEBOARD HID THE BUMPS

The continuation of the cold and wet conditions has meant that the spring cultivations have come to a standstill. The fields are too waterlogged for me to spread my enlarged manure heap without the heavy tackle leaving deep ruts in the soft ground. The cows remain tied in the confines of the cowshed as they wait for the first whisper of warmer weather.

I use these chilly, spirit-dampening days to try to catch up with the multitude of odd jobs that pile up around my one-man farm as rapidly as the manure heap. This week I have been using my long-handled broom to dislodge the skeins of dust-laden cobwebs that drape from the crannies and crevices of the cowshed's corrugated roof and rafters. The spiders will be flushed out later with the penetrating jet of the power hose. After that I shall scrape the walls to remove the layer of manure that sticks limpet-like to the lower surfaces until it is softened. After many months accumulation of smuts and smears the windows now look so clean that when I'm milking it makes me wonder if the glass is there at all.

It is not only in the farm buildings that the annual surge of spring cleaning occurs. In the house my wife is busily bustling around cleaning cupboards, cabinets and chests. One by one the drawers are removed and brought into the warmer part of the house. On the living room table the contents are sorted layer by layer and object by object until the bottom is reached. Then there is a long period of nostalgic relaxation as the local paper of some twenty years ago is removed, read and, eventually, relegated to the dustbin. With a new edition to replace it, the objects and garments are returned, while she wonders if and when they will come back into fashion or can be cut up and used for something else. Still, there will be ample opportunity to solve that problem before the drawer is cleaned again.

Larger pieces of furniture are moved away from the wall to sweep the cobwebs from behind. Tell-tale trickles of fine dust, filtering from tiny holes in the plywood backing, show that the woodworm have spread from the old farmhouse timbers and found fresh feeding and breeding grounds. Out comes the specially spouted tin of evil smelling fluid, and into each orifice is injected a squirt of the obnoxious deterrent, designed to kill and cure the problem in one fell swoop. The furniture is polished and replaced, often in another position just to make a change. 'No, I don't like it there, try it over here'. In some households even the bed rests against a different wall each night, making it very difficult to find your bearings in the early hours!

And so it goes on, until all of it is tidy, the novelty of refurbishing the nest diminishes and more important work comes to hand. The spasm of spring cleaning slowly subsides into the sonorous slumberings of summer. Even so, our springtime misfortunes pale into insignificance when compared with the colossal amount of energy expended by our ancestors.

When the surge struck, farm and cottage walls alike took on a different hue, red, yellow, green or blue - often according to which ochre was left over after marking the 'old tup' the previous autumn. This identifying colourant was mixed with oil and spread on the ram's stomach, so that when he was put with his flock, each ewe that he mated could be noted. The colour was changed every three weeks - on the ram, not the walls!

Layer upon layer of these ancient red-raddles and opaque ochres were used before the advent of cheap wallpaper coverings - and they were difficult to apply. Rolls of wallpaper were sold with a border, which had to be cut away first, either by the shopkeeper (for a small additional charge) with his long sharp scissors and experienced eye, or by a little cutting machine, which on the special occasions that I was allowed to turn the handle for him, usually went wrong and would tear the paper. At other times Mum and Dad cut it themselves at home, but seldom managed to trim it as accurately as the shopkeeper.

The paste was even more perilous. Nothing like the non-stain, easily wash-offable liquid that is made from clear crystals that pour from polythene packets nowadays. They used ordinary white baking flour, boiled in water, sometimes with an addition of alum. This gooey mixture was like a thin porridge and had to be applied very carefully since it would stain the patterned side of the paper wherever it touched.

I m glad I don t have to redecorate my house every spring

Old walls are usually uneven walls, seldom is anything square. Damp and daub don't mix, and replastered patches leave humps and bumps that have to be covered with care - or stand the sideboard in front to hide it! To make rooms look larger the wallpaper often finished a foot or so below the ceiling, over this ragged edge was pasted a narrow horizontal frieze. The ceiling had previously been whitewashed as had the whole of the pantry and dairy. To do this a bucket of quick-lime or several heavy round balls of whiting were slaked in water. When required, this mixture was diluted, stirred and sieved. A pint of 'colostrum', the first milk from a freshly calved cow was added to make it stick, and a swish of the 'blue-bag' to make the whitewash look even whiter.

On wet days when outdoor work was out of the question, it was slapped onto the ceilings and upper parts of the walls with a wide brush - often wielded by inexperienced farmhands, who flirted large blobs of the white sediment in all directions. Furniture was protected by thin white linen covers called dustsheets and the floors with sheets of newspaper. Wall to wall carpeting was not known in those days. The better rooms had a square of carpet in the centre, with extra mats or strips to the doorways and on any part of the carpet that had to take excessive wear.

Cleaning carpets was an ordeal in itself. On a dry day, the carpet was rolled up. If you were posh and could afford it, the underfelt was also removed. If not, the layers of brown parcel wrapping paper were collected. Mum scrubbed the floor, while Dad and I hung the carpet over the linen line - which would often snap under the strain. Now came the demonstration of muscular prowess. The looped oriental cane carpet beater was thumped hard and repeatedly against the carpet's canvas backing, sending thick clouds of choking dust drifting downward. My tiny arms soon tired and Dad took over the task. He hit each area evenly, methodically and rhythmically from top to bottom and from side to side. When eventually the dust diminished the carpet was dragged, pattern side down, across the lawn to renew the pile - after any stray heaps of dog dung had been removed.

By this time the scrubbed floor had dried. Fresh sheets of paper lined the area covered by the carpet, which was put down a different way round, to even out the wear. After the 9 o'clock news my sister and I were sent to bed. Mum and Dad rolled back the four edges of the carpet and 'Darkaline' stained the surrounding floor to the skirting-boards, not forgetting to leave the piece by the door until last, as they left to go to bed. Hopefully by morning the varnish would be dry, the room would look spick and span and be as clean as a new pin.

What a performance it used to be! Yet each year that urge still comes to redecorate the nest. My daughter has spent much of her time during the past few weeks sorting and re-arranging her home. On Easter Monday she presented my wife and I with our first grand-daughter, Claire Emma, who weighed in at six and a half pounds. I expect that's why she had that urge to get on with the spring cleaning.

But I've just been thinking; when I started to write this my wife said she was going to straighten the junk-room. I think I'd better go and see what she's up to! I can understand her sorting through the cupboards and the china-cabinet, but when it comes to the junk-room, I'm beginning to wonder why. After all, as they say, there's many a slip betwixt the cup and the lip!

24 May

BECOME YOUR OWN WATER DIVINER. ALL YOU
NEED ARE TWO COAT HANGERS

It is well into May and today we have some slightly
warmer south-westerly winds. A welcome relief after
one of the coldest and wettest Aprils for many a long
year. But the signs are not yet those of summer. From
their respective pens around the garden the cockerels
have been crowing continuously all morning. For
the past hour or so a thrush has been pairing his
territorial trills from his precarious perch on a
dead twig at the top of the pear tree, as he sings each
song twice over. Opposite my window, on the slope above the
meandering river, three different ages of rabbits are energetically nibbling away at the
fresh green sward. By the back door some of our cats are soaking up the sunshine, while
they wash behind their ears with their paws. Taken individually these sights and sounds
might mean little to most people but, taking them together, and all happening before
mid-day, to the countryman they are a sure sign of more wet and cold weather on the
way.

My cows, usually among the first in the district to be turned out full time, are still
housed at night. Most of my neighbours have turned their stock out to grass out of
necessity, since they have no silage left in the silos. There are dangers in turning cattle
on to lush, wet, young grass too soon. The highly nutritious growth goes through them
like a dose of salts, with nothing to impede its progress. This can cause trouble in cold
and wet conditions when, coupled with a seasonal shortage of magnesium, it causes a
disorder, known as 'Staggers'. The cow acts as if it were drunk and can collapse into a
coma and die, if not treated promptly. As my cows are still having hay at night, this
helps to slow down the rate at which their daytime grazing is digested. Hopefully, this
will make them less likely to succumb to such stress.

Another serious drawback is that grass, grazed too early, does not have sufficient
root reserves and takes longer to recover. Some farmers may well find that once the
cows have creamed off the first flush of growth, a continuing cold and wet spell will
produce poorer pastures in a few weeks' time. We shall just have to hope that doesn't
happen as the greatest gallonage of milk is produced between the middle of May and
the middle of June.

It is not only livestock farmers who have been swamped with problems caused by
the continuing deluge. A lot of arable fields are still waiting to be sown, they are simply
too cold and sticky for seeds to survive. Corn sown in May is usually called 'Cuckoo
Corn' - sown to the call of the cuckoo. And because its growing season is reduced by

two months, the resulting yield is frequently poor and, according to our seers, 'It often won't even pay its way'. On other fields, some already sown, are large lakes of surface water. There can be several reasons for this. Fewer folk on our farms means less time can be spared for routine maintenance. The labyrinth of underground drains are not inspected, rodded and cleaned as in the past and silt or tree roots (especially Willow) clog the pipes.

Sometimes the water cannot percolate to the drains because lack of humus or bad husbandry have killed the worms that aerate the soil and it has become sour and slimy. When used at too high a speed, or when the land is too wet, tractor tyres can skid, slip and slurr, turning the soil into an inpenetrable mess. It produces a solid layer (pan) at plough depth, which has to be broken up with a sub-soiler, before it will allow the water through.

The most frequent cause of wet patches is when a heavy trailer wheel crushes a clay drainpipe or tilts it out of alignment. The whole system stalls to a standstill, backs up the pipe and waterlogs the area. Many of these drainage schemes were put in during Victorian times, when horses and oxen cultivated the land, ploughing was shallow, labour was cheap - and frequently Irish.

Farmers and smallholders who couldn't afford the cost of locally made horseshoe shaped or rounded, baked-clay pipes made their own drainage system. They coppiced long faggots of ash and hazel brushwood from their hedgerows and laid them underground in place of pipes. They have already lasted more than one hundred years and some are still going strong. But if you dig down to find the pipe, all you will ever see is a darkened patch of soil, perforated with tiny holes!

Should you wish to discover where your drainage runs underground across your garden or in the field, here is the simplest and easiest way I know.

All you need are two lengths of metal rod, each bent to an L shape. Brazing rods are ideal, but an easily found alternative is a pair of wire coat hangers. Cut them in two places, an inch (2½ cm) from the hook on one side and an inch above the corner on the other side. Throw away the hook. Bend the short length at right angles to the longer length and close the corner loop as a safety precaution.

To use: Grip the short lengths, one in each hand, with the longer part dipping slightly downwards. Hold them in front of you about a foot (30 cms) apart, with the horizontal bar about an inch above your fingers, so that they can swing freely. Starting with the two rods parallel to one another - 'walkies' - move slowly and steadily forward over a known drain. If the rods come together and cross over, walk on another yard or two, turn round, relax, reposition the rods parallel again and do the return journey. If they crossed for you the first time they should cross again, though not necessarily in the same place. To find the position of the drain, walk over it in both directions, marking the ground where the rods cross. The drain is mid-way between those two marks, and for a fortunate few it will be half that same distance underground. If the rods haven't crossed for you - I'm sorry, but you probably aren't divine!

It works for two out of every three people. But please, please remember that looped end or an enquiring kiddie could run into them and lose his sight. Remember, practice makes perfect, and apply your 'dowsing' - for that is what it is called - with a little bit of common sense. The old drainage systems usually snaked along the natural hollows. New instalments seldom show on the surface. Drains run downhill and be careful if you dig down to find the one in your front garden. Your 'drain' might just turn out to be the electricity cable and if you hit that with your spade, you may be in for a shock!

Anyhow, you should have no shortage of water to search for. Deep purply-blue banks of cloud covered the sun a few minutes ago. Those distant rumbles of thunder are now almost overhead. The cockerels, rabbit, cats and thrush were right; it's pouring down again. We're back to normal - well at least the weather is.

25 June Nature's Nutrients
CURE-ALLS THAT BLOOM IN THE SPRING......AND THE PLANT THAT'S A WEE BIT NAUGHTY!

However unkind the weather, this year will certainly be remembered by many as the year of the blossom. Seldom before have I seen such a riot of colour around the countryside. Opposite my window, all along the sloping river bank, the hue has gradually changed from the earlier golden trumpets of the daffodils to the heavy haze of bluebells. Although I cannot think of any modern use for bluebells, other than perfume, they were once highly valued by 'Fletchers'. They boiled the bulbs to make a glue which was strong enough to fasten goose flight feathers onto the ends of arrowshafts - hence arrowflights.

As the blues of the banks and woods slowly subsided, it was followed in the fields and on the roadside verges by masses of golden dandelions 'the sunflower of spring'. Its original name Dent-de-lion means lion's tooth (dentures of lion), which comes either from the notched edges of the leaves or the multi-fanged tap roots, I must confess, I'm not sure which. The plant is as rich in cures to the herbalist, as it is to 'yours truly' in tales to tell. Its juices were well known to the ancient Greeks, who praised its virtues for curing eye disorders. Nowadays the flowers are generally gathered by amateur winemakers, at mid-day when the sun is shining for the best results. They used to be carefully collected by complexion conscious country maidens. A handful boiled for half an hour made a toilet water which would wash away freckles, if used regularly, night and morning.

Its young leaves are excellent in salads and will rid the body of impurities after winter's ills, relieving jaundice, rheumatism and gout, among others. But a word of warning. When I was a young whippersnapper I was told that eating dandelions would make me want to wee. And, true enough, when I grew older I discovered that the old country name for it was 'Piss a bed'! So take my advice and be ready to run.

In Eastern bloc countries dandelions are cultivated on a large scale as a farm crop. The milky sap is used as a latex to make rubber, and most Russian cars run on dandelion tyres - perhaps it helps them to get there faster! Another of the dandelion's curative attributes was achieved by smearing the milky fluid on to warts, forming a covering seal when dry. The warts would soon shrivel and disappear. It is doubtful whether Oliver Cromwell was ever told about this remedy as he wished his portrait to be painted for posterity 'warts and all'.

There are at least two other country names for this herb, 'peasant's clock' and 'priest's crown'. After a few days the golden flowerballs change to white 'blow-balls', which I used to spend hours blowing to tell the time, whilst older schoolgirls blew the parachute attached seeds away to forecast the years before their marriage.

The white flecking of the fields continued with the coming into flower of the daisy. This humble plant, despised by so many, is in fact a factory of great service to the soil. It manufactures lime and so lessens the acidity around it allowing other plants to thrive. Its name comes from the 'Day's Eye', since by tradition the flowers are supposed to open as the sun rises and close as it sets. Eaten raw, daisy leaves purify the system, ease rheumatism and help allay skin disorders.

As schoolchildren we lads used to puncture daisy stems with our thumbnails, push another stem through the slit and eventually end up with a daisy chain garland for the girl of our choice. They in turn pulled the pink topped petals from the flower head saying "he loves me, he loves me not", always hoping to finish on the last petal with "he loves me"!

Swiftly over the heads of the daisies blooms a mint of golden knots of buttercups. These flowers used to be rubbed onto cows' udders to increase the quantity and improve the quality of the milk. If the bright flower was held under your chin and your skin reflected the yellow - you liked butter!

And now the hedgerow hawthorns have become like mountain glaciers, as avalanches of white cymes cascade along the drooping branches. All around them during every available daylight hour is heard the soothing sound of the murmuring of innumerable bees. If all this blossom should pollinate, set and grow into berries, then the weather prospect for next winter will be very bad indeed, for many berries foretell a hard winter.

Hawthorn (or May) is often called the 'bread and cheese' tree, because the tender tips of the branches are nutritious to nibble. The tips also taste good in salads and are an even safer remedy against heart disorders than the usually recommended 'digitalis' - foxglove (little folks' glove). People who are superstitious say that neither red nor white May blossom (hawthorn) should be taken into hospitals, houses or churches, as its colours are those of blood and bandages. If so used, it becomes an omen of death.

Recently scientists have rediscovered what country people have known for centuries, that the heavy scent (Trimethelamine) is similar to that given off by the recently departed. That is why our ancestors deemed it unlucky to bring hawthorn blossom into an enclosed area. It reminded them, both by colour and smell, of death! I wonder if we should tell that to the bees?

One of my farm jobs this week has been to scythe the roadside nettles. They are smothering and killing the lower branches of my hawthorn hedges. I like to leave clumps of nettles for the butterflies to feed upon. My cows also relish them.

Nettles have a whole host of country uses. Their tender young shoots will make a delicious springtime soup. Whilst their leaves, dried and infused like tea, helped people suffering from anaemia, diabetes, dropsy and rheumatism. History tells us that rheumaticky Romans whipped their aching joints with nettles to soothe the pain - a practice which is still widely recommended, but few seem willing to try it!

Nettles have played a special part in the history of Cheshire - the Cheese Shire. The juice was used instead of rennet to curdle milk, and dairy utensils were cleansed with nettles before the advent of detergents. Chopped leaves, mixed with mash, made

poultry lay more eggs, pigs fatten faster, horses become more frisky and it put a 'bloom' on the coats of both cattle and horses. Nettle stems were steeped in the same way as flax and hemp. The fibres were used for making a coarse cloth, ropes and nets for fishing and rabbit catching - that is why we have the name nettle, because they were used to make nets.

One thing I did notice was that the nettles were acting as host to hordes of aphids - greenfly - come some warmer weather we may well become inundated with these pests. Still, more about them another time perhaps, until then enjoy all those beautiful colours of the countryside - before the greenfly consume them!

26 July
HAYSTACKS THAT GO UP IN SMOKE

One of the saddest sights that a farmer can experience while haymaking is to see the matured swaths of sun-dried grass suddenly soaked by a passing storm. That's what happened to me last week. It rained heavily here nearly all afternoon, yet on a nearby farm they had only a few spots and in the next village - none! However, what did damage in one field did good in the rest. For it gave the scorched grass some much appreciated liquid refreshment. And after an extra day's hard work the hay was harvested in excellent order.

An ancient adage says that there is more bad hay made in a good season than in a bad season. The reason is that in a cold and wet time the farmer makes sure that his crop is completely dry before he bales it. Whereas, in a hot season, the outside surfaces of the stems dry rapidly and become bleached. What is so deceiving is the large amount of sap that remains stored in the stems. Until this has evaporated the hay bales will be green and heavy and if stored in this condition can cause spontaneous combustion. What's that, you ask? Well that's when the stacked grass generates sufficient internal heat to drive out the internal moisture. It still has a supply of oxygen available and continues to overheat itself. Eventually it reaches a temperature where it bursts into flames without any outside interference.

An old farmworker who used to help me on my farm in Shropshire told me how an isolated stack on some low lying meadows had suddenly gone up in smoke one night. He reckoned it was because the hay had been carted too damp, causing spontaneous combustion some two or three weeks later. But the farmer claimed it was caused by a courting couple's cigarettes, that way he could claim the fire insurance for it.

Nearly every countryman has heard the story about the man going to fetch a load of hay in the winter time, slicing into the stack with a hay knife and falling in. The whole of the interior of the stack had smouldered to ashes, leaving only the outside intact.

If I am ever in any doubt about the quality of the hay, either in my earlier years when it was carted and stacked loosely, or nowadays when it is compressed into bales, I leave a chimney hole all the way up the middle of the stack. This is easily done by having a sack of hay which is pulled upwards as the stack is built, leaving a central ventilation shaft. On many occasions, on a cool, still, damp morning, I have seen the steam rising from the ricks and the bales in the barn. All hay should warm up and sweat after stacking. Sometimes I have sweated as much as the hay if it was getting too hot! To test the temperature I push a long iron bar into the stack and leave it for a few minutes. If on withdrawal it is too hot to handle - dial 999 and ask for the fire brigade! If it hasn't quite reached that stage the alternative is to shift the stack, let the air in, and, hopefully, avoid the combustion. I've only ever moved one hot stack - a neighbour's - and I never want to do another. A Turkish bath just isn't in the same league.

Sweating matures the hay and makes it much more palatable to livestock. It also gives the added bonus that I have been enjoying so much this year - the sweet aroma of newly made hay, filling the farmyard with the essence of the countryside as it wafts in whispers on the all too occasional breeze.

The rate at which farmers are turning over to silage makes me think that haymaking may soon become a dying art. They may have taken the sting out of the weather in a wet season, by putting the green grass into airtight clamps or black polythene bags to prevent combustion, but the silage causes as many problems as it solves. Only a few years ago everyone - farmer and smallholder alike - made the bulk of their winter fodder from hay. After a wet spell we were all making hay as soon as the sun shone and literally queuing up for the baling contractor - this year I'm his only customer! The big farms now make silage, the smallholders have gone to the wall, sold

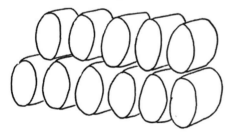

out or died out. The horsey people who have largely replaced them, haven't the tackle or the know-how to make hay on their few acres. They have to buy it at exorbitant prices at the local auction market in winter. It's a strange old world, isn't it? I have learnt from past experience that I would rather push one barrow load of hay to my stock than three times the weight of silage.

Well it's 11 am, the dew has gone off the grass, the sun is shining, it's already 80°F in the shade. My last field of hay has just been cut, thunderstorms are threatened for the weekend. I'm off to get my hay in before the next shower arrives. I don't want to see any more storm soaked swaths this season!

WHEN A GROOM CLOBBERS THE BRIDE WITH A SLIPPER TO SHOW HE'S BOSS

There's nothing more sentimental than a good country wedding, is there? It's strange how life in the countryside seems to rotate in cycles. It was on the same day, nearly twenty-five years ago, that both my neighbour and I took possession of our tenancies and moved into our respective farms. During the past quarter of a century we have established our roots, stabilised our farming enterprises and raised our families. Now our offspring are of that age when they wish to leave home and seek fresh woods and pastures new! So it was that my wife and I were invited to attend the wedding of my next door neighbour's daughter.

I spent much of that hot morning removing the dried dung pats that my cows had deposited from the tarmac pathway along the bottom of the church drive; also sweeping the loose manure from around the gateway of the field which I lend for car parking on such occasions. As the guests started to arrive I closed the further field gates to confine the cows, who were contentedly chewing their cud, whilst basking in the sunshine. I thought of the old saying 'happy is the bride that the sun shines upon'.

She arrived a few minutes late, as is her privilege, in a magnificent 'Brougham', a four-wheeled horse-drawn covered carriage, to the enthralment of as many well wishers outside the church as there were guests packed inside. The service was simple and homely. As the parson explained in his  address - he hadn't married them, they had married each other - for better or worse. Life wouldn't always be a bed of roses, pots and pans might sometimes fly and they had either got to learn to duck, or learn to give and take, to make their marriage a partnership and not a dictatorship.

The register was signed and the bride and groom, now husband and wife, left the church under the archway of her fellow choir members' ancient and modern hymn books. The cameras clicked, the confetti fluttered and, as the carriage conveyed the newlyweds to the reception, I wondered how many people present knew anything of the origins of our ancient wedding etiquette and its quaint customs. Most of them merge into the mists of time, long since past.

HAVE AS MANY CHILDREN AS GRAINS.....

One local tradition is said to have begun when King Canute was passing through the ford at Canute's ford - Knutsford. He got some sand in his shoes. As he was shaking it out a wedding procession passed by. He wished the happy couple as many children as there were grains of sand in his shoes. Since then the doorsteps of the bride and her friends' houses and parts of the road leading to Knutsford church have been 'sanded' on their wedding day. A base layer of dark sand was laid first. Then local white and coloured sands, purchased in one cwt bags from the Macclesfield stone masons, were skilfully funnelled into intricate patterns, scrolls and flowers through a 'tun' dish - a funnel. They often included the motto:

Long may they live, happy may they be.
Blessed with contentment, and from misfortune free.

Any young girl in the Peover parish who wished to become a farmer's wife had first to prove her fitness to churn the milk by lifting the heavy lid of the church chest with one hand. On her wedding day she might well be presented with a bright new heavy George III 'butter penny'. This was for her to add to the 'pundstan' (poundstone) on the butter scales, so that no one could accuse her of selling her produce short weight at the local markets.

Often the bride and groom were too poor to afford to set up home together. To help them the churchwardens would organise a Bride-Ale in the church. The parishioners provided the ingredients, the bride's family brewed the ale and the wardens set the barrels up in church for the occasion. To enter the church you paid one penny if poor and two pennies if rich. Once inside you could drink to your heart's content, it cost no more to drink a gallon than a pint. The money gathered was given to the happy couple. To honour the occasion the bride wore a special outfit called the Bride-Ale gown, and from which the bridal gown of today gets its name!

When, at a later date (1700s), church buildings were used only for religious purposes and not as community centres, the bride would distribute her ale from casks on a cart - the 'Bride-Wain', which trundled around the parish. People would place gifts of corn, wool, utensils, furniture and linen into it as it passed. The local band played on it to encourage everyone to give and so obtain free ale. All and sundry joined the 'band-wagon' to toast the health of the bride and groom. Probably by the next morning many wished they had followed the water wagon instead!

In church the bride's father now gives his daughter's hand in marriage to the groom. In Saxon times the father handed over the bride's slipper to signify the transfer of authority. The husband then bopped his bride over the head with it to symbolise that he was the new master. Over the years slippers changed to shoes and then to boots. So perhaps it is a good job that the custom of hitting her over the head has died out, or a few brides might have died out too! From the wedding night onwards the slipper was

hung over their bed as a symbol of authority. Over his side while he ruled the roost, or over her side if he became a henpecked husband. I wonder - on which side would your slipper hang if this custom had continued?

The church service completed, it was the parson's privilege to be the first to kiss the bride, after which the bride and groom were presented with bags of nuts by well wishers. These foretold plenty of children, especially boys. Others would throw handfuls of wheat with the words 'Bread for life and pudding for ever' or 'May you be as fruitful as the corn'. When families migrated from the countryside and moved into the towns they couldn't buy wheat grains, only processed flour. So they used the nearest alternative - rice - as a substitute. This too became more expensive - and dangerous - when the brown husks were removed and only white rice grains were sold. Not to be outdone, people replaced them with paper shapes, rose petals, hearts and horseshoes, symbols of happiness, good luck and fertility - our present day confetti.

Poor people used to get married early in the morning, work normally all day and have their wedding breakfast in the evening. The rich spent longer over their festivities - they usually covered three days. Family on the first, friends on the second and their workers and servants on the third - to clear up the remnants.

For a period of twenty-eight days (one moon) after the nuptial rituals were over, the newlyweds would supplement their diet with honey, to make them more likely to conceive. That was the original purpose of a honeymoon - and it usually resulted in the twenty-five year cycle revolving all over again!

28 September
WHEN GEESE TREKKED TO MARKET - WEARING SHOES!

Tenant farmers know only too well that St.Michael's Day, 29th September, is when the rent falls due. It used to be the custom that a goose was also handed over in part-payment for your tenancy. Often this was a 'Wayzgoose' - one that had been fattened on the corn stubbles. After payment, the tenants sat down to a goose dinner, provided by the landlord. And, as another rhyme reminds us :

> Whosoever eats goose on St.Michael's Day,
> Shall never lack money his debts to pay.

So, perhaps the landlord was only hedging his bets!

If, when you ate to the wishbone, it was light in colour, it forecast a mild winter, whilst a dark wishbone foretold a harsh winter ahead. An even older narrative said that geese sacrificed at Michaelmas increased the fertility of crops and livestock, and when eaten improved the possibility of producing children. That is why they were once such popular presents for newlyweds.

Severe penalties were imposed on anyone caught stealing geese. Yet no such restraint was inflicted on the wealthy landowners who gradually enclosed the commons, added them to their estates, and so deprived the villagers of their customary grazing rights. As another adage says :

> The law doth punish both man and woman,
> That steals the goose from off the common.
> But lets the greater felon loose,
> That steals the common from the goose.

Around about 1800 William Cobbett wrote that in one six-mile journey in Surrey he counted 'not less than ten thousand geese on the commons'. Every smallholder had a share of the common according to how much land he cultivated. The grazing rule was, one cow is equal to three sheep or nine geese. Any villager with a common grazing right of one sheep could, as an alternative, graze three geese. They were often loosed out in a morning to fend for themselves. Their attendant gander protected them during the day and brought them home at night. For breeding, the best ratio was reckoned to be three geese to each gander:

> On Candlemas Day (2nd February) the good housewife's goose will start to lay.
> On Valentines' Day (14th February) yours and mine may!

The good housewife's goose would lay a hundred or more eggs in a season. If broody, she sat her clutch of eggs for twenty-eight days before the goslings hatched. During that period she didnt favour the affections of the gander. He became restless and wandered aimlessly around the nesting area completely at a loose end and frequently payed his attentions to other attractive females. Consequently, in bygone days, the month after a wife's confinement was called the 'Gander month', when some husbands went 'Gandermooning', for twenty-eight days, or playing the gallant.

In the days before the lawnmower, geese kept the coarser weeds and grasses under control that other poultry passed over, especially cleavers - 'sticky bobs' or 'goosegrass' as it is commonly called. Any errant goose that wandered too often into the kitchen soon found a place in the pot! If penned in summer they were fattened on surplus garden produce, such as lettuces, especially those that had gone to seed (bolted). They ate the remnants of the spring and summer cabbages and, if also fed a small quantity of oats, would readily put on weight to make a cheap and tasty dish when cooked.

In the market place goose meat was on a par with mutton. They both sold at the same price per pound. But it was not only for their meat that geese were bred. Their down was highly valued for filling pillows, cushions and bedcovers, their small feathers for bolsters and mattresses and their thick wing feathers for making quill pens.

According to the Rev. William Daniel, writing in 'Rural Sports' 1807: 'Geese were plucked five times a year. The first plucking is at Lady Day (25th March) for feathers and quills and the same is renewed, for feathers only, four times more between that and Michaelmas. The old geese submit quietly to the operation but the young ones are noisy and unruly.'

Quills were first dried in the oven, then sharpened using a special knife with a folding blade which could be carried in the pocket - a pen knife. People who could write were called 'clerks', an honourable profession in bygone days. Because priests could both read and write they still carry the title 'Clerk in Holy Orders'. But do you know why people who have the surname Clerk or Clarke are usually referred to as 'knobby'? It is because the constant pressure of holding a small diameter quill pen soon caused their ancestors' knuckle joints to become knobbly with arthritis. It became the symbol of their profession to have knobbly knuckles. So people called them 'Knobby the Clerk', hence 'Knobby Clarke'.

Michaelmas Day was also the time of the hiring fairs, when, in addition to hiring hands for farmwork, both farmers and villagers sold their surplus stock. Drovers who bought the animals and birds walked them to larger fairs or to the main centres of population to fatten for Christmas. Large flocks of geese were walked about four miles each day. Four days walking then one day's rest, and so on. Distances of one to two hundred miles were often undertaken, but there was a problem.

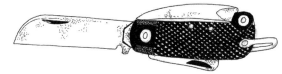

Geese have webbed feet and constant walking could cause blisters which would mean that they rapidly lost condition, so they had to be shoed! Although thought of as a music hall joke, it was once as widely practised, as it was easily performed. The flocks of geese were driven through alternate patches of warm tar and sand. Each webbed foot would be protected by a cushion of tar and sand, tar and sand, which would last for about a hundred miles before it peeled off and they needed reshoeing. They were often reshoed at Nottingham - famous for its goose fairs. If they had to travel long distances, the journey might take forty to sixty days. It would be the end of November before they reached London.

How were they fattened fast enough for Christmas? They were 'crammed' in semi-darkness. Their movements were restricted, either by putting them tightly together in rows and nailing their webbed feet to the wooden floor, or placing several together inside a wooden cask, in which holes had been bored at one end, through which they thrust their heads to be fed. They were force-fed several times a day, by inserting a funnel into their gullet and pouring in a sloppy barley, bean and maize meal mash mixed with milk.

As geese are such voracious feeders they soon fatten and can double their weight within a month to kill out between twenty-four and thirty pounds by Christmas Eve. One lasting delicacy of cram-fed geese is the liver, which weights up to two pounds, and is made into 'pate-de-foie gras' even to this day. About five pounds. of fat could also be collected when you cooked your goose. It was stored in jars until it was needed, then added to the vegetable broth, to keep away winter's ills and chills, massaged onto aching joints and limbs to ease the pain, or rubbed on the chest to keep children free from colds. It was so penetrating that it was claimed it would even soften iron.

In my earlier farming days, I always used it on any cow's udder that had become bruised or inflamed. But few geese are kept in the countryside now, as they don't fit in with factory farming methods. My neighbour did have two that acted as watchdogs around his home last year and we named them Hiss and Honk. But a greasy goose goes down easier than a dry turkey, and they went the way of many other of our feathered friends - in the pot at Christmas.

My rent day is rapidly approaching, but somehow I don't think that my gesture would be appreciated if I paid part of my rent with GEESE!

29 October Witches Bewitched
CHARMS THAT PUT WITCHES TO FLIGHT

Few people today seriously believe in witchcraft. Yet many of the signs, symbols, sayings and superstitions associated with past beliefs linger on in our countryside.

Firmly fastened to the door of many an old out-building or stable is a horseshoe. Nowadays, it is recognised as the symbol of good luck. Most people think that its luck is connected with its shape - that of a crescent moon. Before she arose and after she set, the moon goddess was called 'Hecate' - the guardian of all doors and entrances.

LUCK RUNS OUT

But there is a far wider yet less known reason for using the horseshoe as a symbol to avert evil and bring good luck. When the Celts from Northern Europe invaded and conquered our country, they did so largely because they had tools and weapons of a much superior metal - iron. People thought that iron was like a God because it possessed such powerful properties. They wished to own some of this magical metal to ward off their enemies, witches and evil spirits. But iron was both rare and expensive, only the very rich could afford it. However, if you were a poor peasant and you happened to be walking along where a horse had cast its shoe, there was a free piece of iron - the luck of the gods was on your side!

CATCH YOUR LUCK

So, the horseshoe became the symbol of good luck - because it was made of iron. By hanging it on the stable door it prevented witches and evil spirits casting their spells on the animals inside. During the 16th and 17th centuries the spells of any visitor would be nullified if a pair of (iron) scissors, opened to form a cross, was hidden under the cushion of the chair in which she was invited to sit. This power of the cross is still invoked today when we cross our fingers!

Our ancestors believed that ash was an anti-witch wood. Ash lintels were used over the doors, windows and chimney openings to prevent the witch gaining access to the house. A rowan tree grew near the door for the same purpose - its other name is the mountain ash. Another deterrent was salt, sealed in a glass tube, buried within the wattle and covered with daub because it was believed the witch would have to count every grain before she could enter. A curious alliance combining a belief in the power of the church, iron and salt occurred in the Bellamine jars. These wine jugs originated from the Rhineland. An embossed bust of the grey bearded Catholic Cardinal Bellamine appeared on the narrow neck of each bottle. Urine from each member of the household was poured inside onto pins, nail clippings and hair cuttings. This was heated on the fire until it spluttered. The bottle was corked and buried upside down under the doorstep or the hearthstone. This enactment was said to break any spells that had already been cast and cause the witch to confess. It would also guard the house whenever its occupants were absent.

It was simply a later version of the much earlier custom of burying the deceased head of the household under the hearthstone so that his spirit would help to protect the property. 'Corn dollies', which rattled in the breeze were hung from the eaves of stacks to prevent witches gaining access and spoiling the corn. Curtains on four poster beds were fastened with cords ending with a tassel. It was thought that the witch would so enjoy playing with your tassel that she would pass no further and you would enjoy a good night's sleep.

Blacksmith's aprons, shawls, ecclesiastical garments and church embroideries had border fringes in which witches and evil spirits would become entangled should they try to pass 'beyond the fringe'. Round 'witching baubles' of silvered glass (similar to those we hang on the Christmas tree) were hung at vantage points around the house. Their purpose was to reflect any spells back onto the sender. Silver was widely used as a deterrent against witches. 'Cross my palm with silver' says the gypsy before telling your fortune. This originated because they were often accused of witchcraft. To make the sign of the cross on her left palm with a silver coin was something a witch could not endure. That was the gypsy's way of proving her innocence - and obtaining your money!

To stop babies of the wealthy becoming bewitched, their godparents presented them with a silver spoon at their christening, so that when they were being spoon fed during their formative years, any spells put upon them were nullified by the reflection of the silver. To 'be born with a silver spoon in your mouth' meant you were blessed with good luck, hereditary wealth, or both, from birth. In the 16th century these spoons obtained the additional blessing of the Christian church by depicting an 'apostle' on the end of each handle. The complete set was twelve 'apostle spoons' - was that the reason they had such big families in bygone days - to get a full set of spoons?

Another name for a witch was a hag. One of the most powerful potents against her magic was the 'hagstone'. This was a stone with a natural hole through the centre - it represented the pupil of the 'all seeing eye'. It was once widely believed that, at night, witches would gallop across the heavens on horseback to visit their associates in the next world. Sometimes when the horseman went to tend his steed early in the morning he would find it trembling and all of a lather - sweating, its mane and tail tied in knots. He thought the witch had just returned it after a night of hard riding, in other words it had been hag-ridden. His remedy was to keep the horse in the stable for three days without food, but under the influence of the hagstone, hung just above it, then the witch wouldn't be able to ride that horse for the rest of the season. Today veterinary surgeons would explain that the horse was suffering from 'Monday morning fever' - 'Lymphanitis' the swelling of the lymph glands. It had eaten too much and not done enough work to get rid of its surplus energy. The cure - less food and more work.

This ailment doesn't only apply to horses. Monday morning fever happens to the human race as well! Witches were also thought to take sleeping children with them on some of their excursions. This might explain why, perhaps in the early hours of the morning, your child may have wakened you by screaming 'Mum, Mum, help Mum, Mum (never Dad, Dad!). You go to soothe your offspring, who is trembling, sweating, and feverish. What kind of a dream do you say that they have had? Yes, that's right a 'night-mare'. They've been hag-ridden, so what was the remedy? Hang a hagstone over the bed and keep them without food for three days because, according to the time honoured saying ' you feed a cold but starve a fever'!

And these are only a few of the very many signs, symbols, sayings and superstitions about witchcraft that are still in current use today.

30 November 'Goose-Summer' Spiders
IT'S TIME FOR SPIDERS TO START HANG-GLIDING

The months move forward from the mellow mists and fruitfulness of the earth's October harvest. They give way to the freezing fogs and shrouded silence of November's scenic splendour. The trees slowly lose their chlorophyll cloaks of green. For a few delightful days they - like Joseph - are clothed in an amazing technicolour dreamcoat of autumnal hues. Then little wisps of wind whirl the leaves from the trees to litter the fields with Nature's natural fertiliser.

Dawdling children on their way home from school wade through deep drifts of rustling leaves, kicking them hither and thither. Gardeners rake them into piles and fill high-sided barrows, then tip them unceremoniously onto the compost heap. Council workmen curse them when they clutter up the gutters and foul the footpaths and drains. Hibernating hedgehogs snuggle into spiky spheres in dry and cosy corners, they wrap themselves inside an insulating, blanketing ball of leaves. Lots of leaves finish up as food for worms. They pull them down their holes and after bacterial breakdown the decomposed leaves act as a future foodstore.

In both field and garden the gossamer spiders spin their silken strands which cover the fallen leaves and grass with a shining carpet of silvery threads that glimmer and glisten, glint and gleam in the shimmering shafts of sunlight. And so on, and so on! How lovely to wax lyrical. But to pass from the poetical to the practical. I was astounded to discover that there are about two million spiders on every acre of established pasture. At this time of the year, the parents send their youngsters packing. Although it may be the age of the train, some young spiders appreciate the advantage of aviation. Waiting for a warm, sunny day with just a light breeze, they climb to the topmost tip of a blade of grass. From this vantage point they start to spin long lengths of silken skeins. If the breezes catch them they float upwards and the spider hangs on for dear life. Sometimes the spider only moves a few feet, others, caught in stronger currents drift along on the breeze until the cobweb catches on a hedge, tree or even the barbed wire that surrounds my fields. Some have been found floating in the sky as high as an aircraft can fly. They can travel half way around the world before coming into land. Thus the hang-gliding spider journeys to his new home - airborne.

The old name for an inky-pinky spider was a 'Coppe' and what he wove was a 'coppe-web', now abbreviated to cobweb. By the way, if you are an arachnophobic, it simply means that you are frightened of spiders for, according to Greek mythology, there was once a skilled weaver of tapestries called Arachne. Athene, the powerful goddess of war, learning and the arts was envious of her skill and challenged her to a weaving contest. Both were to design and weave an intricate, beautiful and complex tapestry.

Arachne chose for her subject the signs of the zodiac. When they had both finished the Gods judged the competition and awarded the prize to Arachne. The Goddess Athene was so furious that she immediately cast a spell upon Arachne and changed her into a spider, so that she would have to spin for evermore. Whereupon Arachne hanged herself which is why, even today, you will still see a spider 'hanging' by its single silken thread, to remind us of this legend.

For astrologers Arachne the spider is the thirteenth sign of the zodiac, since she wove the connecting thread that runs through the other twelve symbols.

The word gossamer has two possible origins. Folklore suggests it was a thread from the winding sheet (shroud) which carried the Virgin Mary to heaven. Gods-seam = gossamer. The more logical explanation is that these spiders' webs are more apparent during any fine spell around St. Martin's Day, November 11th, which was once called St. Martin's summer. But, because so many geese were being fattened at this time it was later called Goose-Summer, hence the goose-summer or gossamer spider.

Farmers used to think that 'fog-fever' was caused by cattle eating coarse fog-grass, when it was covered with gossamer cobwebs during damp and foggy conditions. They thought that the spiders' webs tickled the bronchial tubes which made the cattle cough (hoose or husk) and rapidly lose condition. As the infection would quickly weed out any weakly animals, young stock in particular were housed at night and only turned out when the grass was dry. We now know that the husky cough is caused by an organism called a lungworm. This lives irritatingly in the lung, where it lays its eggs. They are coughed up into the mouth and swallowed. They become larvae and live for a month in the intestines, then pass out with the dung on to the pasture. After a week the larvae mature, become infective, climb up a wet blade of grass and wait to be eaten. Once inside an animal's digestive tract it bores through the lining wall, wriggles its way into the lungs and starts laying eggs, and so the cycle continues.

Fortunately, there is now a reliable oral vaccine so, each season, I dose all my young stock twice before ever turning them out onto grass, especially when the goose-summer spiders are weaving their webs!

31 December God Speed the Plough
WHY PLOUGH HORSES GALLOPED OFF TO THE PUB

Until comparatively recent times, it was the unalterable law of the land that all ploughing, especially of heavy clay, should be finished before the festive season. The wooden plank that originally turned the furrow was called the 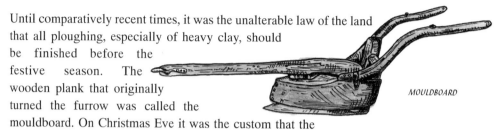 mouldboard. On Christmas Eve it was the custom that the ploughman should remove the mouldboard from his plough, polish it, put it under his bed and 'sleep' on it. And, knowing that his season's work was completed on schedule, he could rest easy and enjoy his Christmastide.

MOULDBOARD

Although at first we may think this custom quaint and humorous, it is, like nearly all other ancient traditions, based on factual farming. The easiest way to deal with the cultivation of the countryside under all weather conditions was only learned from long years of bitter experience. For 'as the days lengthen the cold strengthens'. If the ploughing was completed by Christmas the frost, snow and winds of winter would crumble the clay clods into a fine workable tilth in time for the Spring sowing.

Ploughmen had other customs that were just as religiously observed. On the first Sunday after the Epiphany (First Sunday after twelfth night) a special service was held in the church. The plough, surrounded by farmworkers, was blessed as the symbol of the foundation of the farmer's work and prayers were recited in the hopes of a prosperous harvest to follow. Next morning, on what is now called Plough Monday, the ploughmen would again dress in their best white smocks. But this time they were also embellished with brightly coloured ribbons and horse brasses. They were accompanied by the village 'mummers' in full costume, including 'Bessy' a man dressed as a woman, who carried the collecting box. The newly blessed plough was also bedecked with ribbons.

Instead of being drawn by the normal team of young bullocks (stots), it was pulled by the plough boys, who were consequently nicknamed 'stots'. As their procession came to each farm or smallholding the mummers would act out their customary souling play, based on ancient fertility rites. They were watched eagle-eyed by the farmer, his family, servants and staff. After the applause at the end of the performance, everyone was generously rewarded with hot minced-meat pies, apples, nuts and leftovers from the Christmas festivities. All was swilled down with an abundance of home brewed beer. Most of the hosts would present 'Bessy' with a monetary donation - 'largesse' - to buy extra beer at the pub afterwards. Also an offering to keep the plough light burning in the church sanctuary. For it was widely believed that while the sanctuary lamp burned, good crops would continue but if it failed, famine would follow.

If anyone was too mean to provide victuals for the entertainers or 'largesse' to maintain the lamp, the whole team would 'set to' and plough deep furrows in the footpaths and greensward around his house. The occupant dared not complain, other than verbal abuse, because that was the recognised retribution.

There was always a great deal of friendly rivalry between ploughmen. They spent much of their free time bragging about the craftsmanship of their own work and criticising the work of others. Some would walk miles over a weekend to compare the skill of a particularly well swept furrow with their own handiwork.

A novice whose furrows were as crooked as a dog's hind leg would be chastised by all and sundry, saying 'if a rabbit ran at any speed up that furrow, why, he'd break his neck - twisting and turning around those corners'. To determine just who was the best among them,

they arranged a special competition. On the same day, in the same field, each man was given an area of land to plough within an allotted time. Local landowners and farmers acted as adjudicators. So began what continues today, the challenge of the Ploughing Match.

Throughout the ages ploughmen have been renowned for the accuracy with which they cast their furrow straight. The city of Rome was marked out by ploughmen and it was they, not the legion of surveyors, who were responsible for drawing the centre spit of the long straight lengths of Roman roads. In medieval times they were

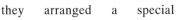

again required to work on the roads. Not to straighten them, but to plough in and level the deep ruts that left the tracks treacherous in winter, with quagmires of mud and slutch, often knee deep.

Oxen were extremely efficient at converting food into energy for work. The females, although not quite as strong as the stots (bullocks), tipped the scales in their favour by providing the farmer with a calf and milk each year. Oxen only needed rough grazing in the summer and straw in the winter. At the end of the their working life they produced a bonus of meat, leather and horn. The main drawback of using cattle for fieldwork was that they were slow and ponderous, needing frequent rest periods - in fact every 220 yards, when ploughing. So fields were sized to accommodate their capabilities, often being made 220 yards in length - or one furrow long - one furlong. The width of the land between the main furrows was one chain = 22 yards = one tenth of the furrow length. The area enclosed by the land width, 22 yards, when multiplied by the furrow length, 220 yards, is 4840 square yards, which is called an acre! When distances became standardised in Elizabethan England, eight furrow lengths became a mile, 1760 yards = 8 furlongs! If the furrow was nine inches wide (23 cms), the ploughman and his team walked eleven miles to turn over each acre of land!

In course of time new breeds of horses were introduced that were faster and stronger at work. They gradually ousted the cumbersome oxen. But once again, change brought its problems. Horses required higher quality foods, good grazing in summer, hay and oats in winter. The whole pattern of agriculture had to change, more grass had to be sown and mown, more hay harvested and more grain grown. Poorer farmers were sometimes conned into buying broken winded ex-government horses because they were cheaper. They bought ex-cavalry chargers or ex-Royal Mail, but these caused a problem. They were trained to respond immediately to the bugle or the horn, and to charge towards the enemy or to gallop to the nearest posting station - usually a pub!

In the winter months fox-hunting was a widespread country sport and woe betide any ploughman who hadn't finished his stint by Christmas. For at the slightest hint of a 'Tally-ho' from the huntsman's horn, the horses would prick up their ears, cock their tails and charge post haste to the nearest pub, the ploughman in hot pursuit after them. Only to find on arrival that inside were the inebriated village mummers, spending the last of their 'largesse'. Happily reciting the centuries old inscription on the side of their beer and cider mugs -

'God Speed the Plough :
Let the wealthy and the great
Roll in splendour and state,
I envy them not I declare it.
I eat my own lamb,
My own chicken and ham,
I sheer my own fleece,
and I wear it.

I have lawns, I have bowers,
I have fruits, I have flowers,
The lark is my morning
                    alarmer.
So jolly boys now,
Here's 'God Speed the Plough',
Long life and success
                    to the Farmer.

32 January 1984 Ice Houses
ICY SECRETS OF THE SPOOKY CELLARS

There must be thousands of them around the countryside. They are hidden in woods and beneath old buildings. I know of at least half a dozen that still exist in this area alone. These spooky cellars sunk in the soil once played an important part in the lives of countryfolk. What is their secret? What purpose did they serve? The answer is that they were .....ICE HOUSES. Nearly every hall had at least one, sometimes two or three. They were large brick-lined underground storage chambers, between ten and twenty feet in diameter and of a similar depth, capped with a domed roof and covered with earth.

In the depths of winter when pits and ponds, lakes and meres were frozen many inches thick, it was the unenviable task of the estate workmen to go 'ICE-TING'. Long before the days of waterproof clothing and wellington boots, 'Ice-ting' was that dreaded, drenching, dangerous job of filling the 'ice-houses'.

First they broke an area of ice at the edge of the pond and backed the special low slung ice cart into the water until its flat bottomed floor was awash. Some of the men had long handled 'Krome' forks, with their tines bent at right angles, to scoop the ice floes into the cart. Others busily broke new lumps away with their sledge hammers. Even though they used long ladders and planks to span the edges of the ice, it was almost inevitable that during the day someone would 'slip' into the icy water - either by accident or devilish design. And, to the derision of the rest, have to hurry home to change into dry clothing.

If the ice was too thick to break with hammers they used cross cut saws and also the two-man pit saw from the estate saw pit. The two men jokingly tossed a coin first to decide whose turn it was to work in the pit underneath! After a hole had been broken through the ice, two separate sawyers cut parallel lines about two feet apart. The long length was broken at the end and the slice was slid upwards onto uncut ice where it was sawn into blocks. These were lifted onto the cart or sledge with long handled two-man ice tongs. Smaller slabs were moved with one-man ice tongs - like large scissor grips; they had either long or short handles.

At Capesthorne, part of the dewpond has a brick flooring to stop the cart sinking into the mud when loaded. To help the horses get a grip on the slippery sloping bank, special chisel or pyramid shaped metal studs were screwed into their shoes. The loaded ice cart was backed to the sloping North facing doorway of the ice-house and tipped. The ice cascaded down into the lantern-lit darkness of the depths below. It landed on an insulating mat of straw overlaying heather and broom, which in turn overlaid sticks to aid any melting ice water to flow freely into the drain. There it was levelled, if in block form it was stacked neatly or if in slabs it was pummelled to exclude the air.

The whole load was covered with an insulating layer of straw, bracken sawdust or moss, especially around the edges. Another load cascaded down; the men underneath only just getting to the far side in time! More levelling, more pummelling, more insulation. The task went on day in and day out until the underground chamber was filled with a gigantic sandwich of ice and insulation. The top doorway was tightly sealed to exclude the air and further layers of straw insulated the space between the inner and outer doors.

Workmen preferred ice-ting when it was freezing hard, then there wasn't as much water dripping off the blocks, they didn't get as wet. If ice was not available the houses were filled with snow. When compressed, first underfoot and then under the weight of snow above, it too solidified into ice. Salt was sometimes added.

When ice-ting, the estate provided the workmen with extra rations of bread, cheese, pickled onions and beer which they ate in the 'bothy' - a small workman's cottage with a roaring fire to thaw out their chilled limbs and set them tingling.

Ice house designs differed widely. Two at North Rode had pyramidal roofs on a timber frame with two openings to allow tipping from either side. One near Stockport is a vaulted cellar under a barn. Others were built like a cavern, cut into the hillside. The ice for these was carried in crates along the tunnel entrance and lowered by block and tackle to be systematically stacked as before. Properly packed and stored the ice would often last for two years, . The secret of success seems to have been in keeping everything as dry as possible and draining any water away immediately. I was once told by someone who had worked in them that in cold weather ice houses felt warm and musty, and in hot weather cold and musty, yet the temperature never varied by more than the odd degree!

But why go to all this trouble, what was the ice used for? Some of our ancestors had enormous appetites. They soon got fed up with produce that had been smoked, salted or pickled to preserve it. Here was a tasty alternative. Fish, game and meat could be stored in them and kept fresh. The wealthy also had insulated freezing boxes installed in their cool north facing pantries. These had a central food compartment, that was surrounded by crushed ice. The ice was topped up with fresh supplies, as required. In midsummer they required attention every two or three days but in midwinter they would often last for a fortnight between fillings. Crushed ice was also used to surround the small tubs in which ice-cream, syllabubs and other frozen delicacies could be whisked and whirled.

NORT.

DRAIN

Before the age of antibiotics, doctors would often prescribe ice packs to be held on the patient's forehead or nape of the neck to reduce temperatures during fevers. They would help to stem haemorrhages or reduce swellings and pains from strains and sprains! The ice was collected, wrapped in layers of flannel, newspaper or in a hay box, from the water bailiff, who was usually in charge of the ice house.

When a foolproof factory method of producing ice in large quantities from purified water was invented, carts and wagons plied the streets of rising suburbia, selling large blocks of dripping ice to fill the cold chests of the 'nouveau riche'. Modern technology has since provided the rest of us with low cost fridges and freezers.

Now the obsolete ice-houses are fenced off, their doorways are bricked up to prevent straying cattle or inquisitive children from falling in. And there they remain, those hidden holes, submerged in the soil - and in the childhood memories of some of our senior citizens.

33 February
SHROVETIDE LEGENDS AND HOW TO TELL SHEEP FROM GOATS

'SHROVETIDE' was formerly a three-day festival and revelry that finished on Shrove Tuesday. In France it was called Mardi Gras, 'Fat Tuesday'. All foods which were forbidden during the forthcoming forty days of Lent and would not keep until Easter, were eaten to save them from being wasted. Slices of meat 'escalopes' gave the name to Collop Monday, whilst on Tuesday, butter and eggs were used up by cooking pancakes.

The ringing of the first pancake bell at 11.30 am signalled the start of the holiday. Workers downed their tools and housewives donned their aprons to fry their pancakes. In some districts the second bell at 11.45 am started the race to be the first at church with a cooked pancake. It had to be tossed three times en route. The winner was rewarded with a kiss from the bell-ringer and a prayer book from the priest.

Before the religious reformation of King Henry VIII, the main purpose of the pancake bell was to call people to confess or 'shrive' their sins, so that they could enter Lent with a clean sheet. This was probably why the season was also called 'Goodtide'.

Fancy that she called me father!

On Shrove Tuesday evening, when all the parishioners had shrived themselves and received absolution, the priest would symbolically transfer all the sins that he had heard into a GOAT. The animal was set free and whipped out of the area by everyone concerned. As the goat escaped it carried their sins away with it, so it was called an Escapegoat - scapegoat! A similar annual ceremony is recorded in the Old Testament on the Day of Atonement

(Leviticus, Chapter 16). Anyone who killed a scapegoat for meat would have to shoulder the additional sins of the community. Every family in turn had to provide the goat for this ceremony, until, according to folklore, one Welsh family was too poor to own a goat and so made a replica out of straw. The complicated plait, traditionally said to represent the goat's head, is now known as the

'Welsh Border Fan'. It is still widely made, and it does resemble a goat's head. But why use a scapegoat, why not a scapesheep! you may ask. From early times goats were associated with the left, the North and the Devil. Sheep with the right, the South and God. The Gospel of St. Matthew, (Chapter 26 verse 22), states that the sheep will be separated onto God's right hand and be welcomed in heaven, and the goats divided to the left will depart into everlasting fire prepared for the devil. Also, before the devil warred with God and was thrown out of heaven, (Revelation 12) he was God's LEFT-hand man! Which is why when you spill salt, the symbol of purity, you throw a pinch over your left shoulder into the face of the devil, with your right hand - three times, signifying the Father, Son and Holy Spirit. The heraldic term and the Latin word for right is dexter and for left - sinister.

Also spun by countless generations of children at this time of year, one of their games has a 'sinister' connection - the whipping top. As the custom of whipping away their sins in the scapegoat declined, it became the duty of each parish to provide a top for whipping on Shrove Tuesday instead. The idea was to expel hardship and evil from the community. Tops were also widely used to try any villager accused of witchcraft, whose name had been placed inside the church witching chest. The top had to be whipped by them. If it spun clockwise (deiseil) they were on God's side, if it spun anti-clockwise (widdershins), they were in league with the devil and would be punished accordingly. The explanation was simply in which hand you held the whip, if in the right hand the top spun clockwise, in your left hand - anti-clockwise.

Even today, in most ceremonials, the article or the participants rotate clockwise, as when passing the port, clipping the church or carrying the coffin! Another quaint reminder of the division between God and the devil - good and evil, left and right, north and south - is still continued in many churches today. At the service of Holy Communion, the Epistle - the letters to the converted Christians - is read from the south side of the altar, God's side. The Gospel; the message of salvation to the Heathen, is read from the north side - the devil's side.

In olden days children were christened in the porch, usually on the south side of the church. The baptised baby was then carried inside to be accepted by the congregation. At the same time the north door of the church was opened to let the exorcised devil escape, which is why the north door is often called the devil's door. People also believed that the devil lurked in the shadows on the north side of the churchyard, so the oldest graves are usually on the south side, God's side.

Children were also connected with another custom on this day. Almost every

THE FULL TOSS!

school owned at least one fighting cock, which was paid for by pennies contributed by the pupils. On Shrove Tuesday they barricaded the school and barred the headmaster until he relented and gave them half a day holiday to attend the local 'Battle Royal'. For this, 16 fighting cocks were paired until the victor emerged, or occasionally all 16 cocks were pitted together, a real 'Battle Royal'.

To cockfighting enthusiasts, Shrove Tuesday was Derby Day, but to farmworkers in Cheshire, Pancake Day was named 'Guttit Day', probably because everyone HAD to eat his or her full quota of pancakes. Anyone failing to do so was put into the wooden wheelbarrow, trundled up the midden plank and tipped out into the manure.

Oh, and by the way, that piece about sorting the sheep from the goats which I mentioned earlier, I have it on good authority that in the Holy Land they look absolutely identical, except to their shepherd. Here, for what it is worth, is one of the ways you and I might tell the difference - simply make them happy! Then the goats will waggle their tails upwards and the sheep will waggle theirs downwards. But I've since been wondering - how do you make them happy in the first place? Thereby hangs a tail!

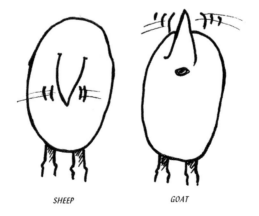

SHEEP   GOAT

34 March Lenten Customs
SWEET END TO OLD COUPLE'S BOILING ROW

Early Spring has always been regarded as the hungriest time of
the year. In past centuries only animals that were required for
working or breeding were kept over the Winter. By now
they would have eaten the larger part of their reserved
rations. And humans, as well as the stock, were starting to
go hungry. No milk was being produced, because the cows
required a rest for a couple of months before calving, to
enable all their available energy to be given to the rapidly

developing unborn calf and the gradual
swelling of the milk bag - the udder. This
process has happened every spring time for hundreds of years
and farmers still call this pre-pregnancy enlargement of the
udder 'springing', even when it occurs in cows
calving at other times of the year!

There were also no eggs to eat because
under natural conditions of feeding and
lighting, poultry stopped laying as the days got
shorter. Then they too had a rest. When the
hours of daylight lengthened sufficiently, their
combs reddened, they started clucking and laid
a clutch of about a dozen eggs. Unless the eggs
were removed regularly the hens would go
broody, they stopped laying and started to
incubate the eggs. The dilemma was that if you
wanted chicks you had to stop eating the eggs -
you couldn't have your eggs and hatch them!

The ploughed fields and the spade dug gardens remained brown
and lifeless, as were the tender tips of the grass and herbs, suffering from
frost scorch and the biting Easterly wind. Nothing was yet growing, for
spring was the season for sowing. People who had put on layers of fat
during the fruitful festivals of Michaelmas, Hallowtide, Martinmas and
Christmas were now having to draw on their reserves and were getting
thinner. Those who were thin at the start of the winter were really feeling
the pinch and many might not survive until the warmer weather. They were all having
to tighten their belts an extra notch or two.

It was largely for these practical reasons that the early Christians chose to
superimpose their beliefs onto this period of the year rather than any other. What better

time to enforce a religious fast than when food was naturally scarce anyhow. The two conditions would complement each other, by eating less through fasting the sparse remaining rations could be eked out a little longer. And from the religious angle, their self denial of animal products could be interpreted as a period of purification for their souls or as a penance for their sins, depending upon which dogma was in vogue at the time.

So, in the fourth century began the 'Lencten-fasten' during the thirty-six lengthening days before Easter. Around 600 AD this was increased to forty days to correspond with our Lord's fast, temptations and wanderings in the wilderness. At about the same time Pope Gregory the Great introduced a ceremony which gave the first day of Lent its name 'ASH Wednesday', when he sprinkled the consecrated ashes, from the palms of the previous year's Palm Sunday, onto the heads of the penitents.

On this day country folk made effigies of a Holly boy and an Ivy maid, who were later burned and the ashes scattered. They also made a straw figure called 'Jack-O'-Lent', who was dressed in old clothes, rather like a scarecrow, and paraded along the country lanes and town streets, before being set up in a prominent position. People would pelt him with sticks and stones at any time during Lent. He was supposed to represent Judas Iscariot, but as he was burned before Easter he probably originally represented the dying winter.

Because meat eating was banned during Lent, fishponds came to the fore. Many inland towns and most monasteries had large ponds or lakes specially flooded to produce a replacement food of fish. But when the monasteries were dissolved by King Henry VIII the fishponds fouled up and went out of production.

In desperation many people went back to eating meat. To counteract this and to encourage the home fishing industry, and also to be able to recruit more seamen in case of emergency, an Act of Parliament in 1562/3 ordered complete abstinence from flesh during Lent and also on Wednesdays, Fridays, Saturdays and Ember Days, under a penalty of three pounds or three months' imprisonment. But the church found a loophole in the law. For a fee of four pence and a tariff based upon the rank of the applicant, a dispensation note could be entered in the church book so that - if your health required it - meat could be eaten on forbidden days. So many licences were issued that the law fell into disrepute, but remained on the Statute Book until 1863!

Half way through Lent comes Mothering Sunday, when all able bodied parishioners were expected to attend their Mother Church, often several miles distant. 'Youngsters' in service, apprenticed to a craft guild, or working on outlying farms, were allowed home for the day. On the way they would gather posies of primroses, wild violets or daffodils (Lenten lilies) for their mothers. Later the local church took the place of the Mother Church. Recently Mothering Sunday has changed to a commercial Americanisation of Mothers Day, when the church is forgotten by most, but mother is remembered with a pot plant or box of chocolates - just when she is in the middle of her Lenten slimming diet!

At our church all the ladies of the congregation receive a posy of flowers and everyone has a piece of traditional simnel cake. The purists will tell you that the word simnel comes from the Latin 'Simila' meaning finest wheat flour. But folklore has it that it probably all began at Bury or Shrewsbury, where there lived an elderly couple, Simon and Nell, who hoped their children would come 'mothering'. The only food they had in the house to offer them was some lenten dough and the remains of the Christmas pudding. The couple agreed to surround the pudding with the dough, but when they thought about cooking it, 'Sim', as she called him, said that it should be boiled and Nell said it should be baked. Neither would back down, words turned to blows, during which the stool and broom got broken. Eventually, exhausted by their efforts they agreed on a compromise.

The cake would first be boiled and then baked, using the wood from the broken broom and stool to kindle the fire. The cake was made and when it was eaten by their children, they declared that it was the best cake they had ever tasted and asked for the recipe. Ever since it has been called a 'Sim-Nel cake' after the kindly old couple who, we are told, never argued again and lived happily after!

But even stranger than folklore is the fact that the forty day period of self denial during Lent only covers the weekdays. Sundays are not included in the fast! If you don't believe that, count them and see - count the days from Ash Wednesday to Easter Day and see how many you get; you may be in for quite a surprise!

35 April Easter Customs
QUAINT CUSTOMS THAT FADE AWAY WHEN MERMAIDS
SANG IN THE LAKE AS THE SUN DANCED

It seems such a shame that so many of the quaint customs of our church and countryside have been allowed to fade away. The origins of some of these ceremonies stretch back to religious beliefs that were widely practised long before the arrival of Christianity or of recorded writings. They acted as stepping stones that marked the passing of the seasons, and gave a symbolic significance to the people who performed them as they journeyed along the perilous pathway of life.

About ten days before Easter country folk would 'Go a palming', gathering greenery to decorate their homes and churches ready for Palm Sunday. Real palm branches like those strewn in front of Jesus on his triumphant ride into Jerusalem had to be imported and were expensive, so country people compromised. They cut branches of evergreen box and yew and gathered long sticks of hazel with its drooping cascades of lambstail catkins, also pussy willow fronds with their furry silver grey buds, capped with yellow pollen, and used them instead.

Small willow trees were also decorated with daffodils. Crosses were plaited from thin whippy rowan branches and hung around the house to avert evil during the coming months. Before Christian times similar branches were carried in procession around the fields. It was claimed they had the power of producing gentle rain to germinate the seeds and of diverting hailstorms that might otherwise have damaged tender shoots. The acknowledged food for Palm Sunday was fig pudding (St. Mark XI), rather like Christmas pudding, but replacing the dried fruit with figs.

Maundy Thursday takes its name from the opening words of the choral antiphon for that day 'Mandatum novum do vobis' (a new commandment give I unto you) and continues with the story of Jesus washing his disciples' feet. Until the reign of James II English monarchs performed this rite as a penance by washing the feet of as many poor people as the years of their age. Then they distributed gifts to the poor from a two-handled wicker basket called a 'Maund'.

Maundy Thursday was also called Chare or Shere Thursday, meaning to clean. Altars were washed spotless by Chareladies (charladies), and the sinful received absolution, which made them clean and free from guilt.

Men had their hair 'schered' and their beards clipped to smarten themselves, ready for the forthcoming festivities. Monks had the tonsure shaved, the remaining short cropped ring of hair (corona) was to remind them and others of our Lord's crown of thorns.

Good Friday was God's Friday. Carpenters would not work on that day as it was their profession that had fashioned the cross, and blacksmiths refused because they had forged the nails that had fastened Christ to the cross. Farmworkers were given the day off to sow their seeds and plant their potatoes, as this was the only day that the devil had no jurisdiction over the soil.

Meanwhile the hard-worked housewife had been busy since dawn preparing batches of small, round, spiced currant buns. As with all yeast cakes and bread, they were individually marked with the sign of the cross to allow the dough to rise and stop the devil getting in and turning them sad (solid). These buns were often taken to church to be blessed before being baked. They had by tradition to be eaten fresh and hot, which is why they are known as Hot Cross Buns. Because they had been consecrated it was thought they would never go mouldy and that they possessed curative powers. So those buns surplus to the immediate requirements of the family were further dried in the oven, then hung from the kitchen ceiling and stored. When anyone was suffering from dysentery, diarrhoea, summer sickness or whooping cough, a sufficient portion of one of the buns was finely grated and mixed with milk or water to make a medicine to cure the ailment. Powdered buns mixed into a warm mash were also given to ailing cattle.

The origin of the hot cross bun goes back two thousand years or more, when similar cakes, divided into four quarters, representing the four phases of the moon, were eaten at the Spring equinox in honour of the Moon Goddess Diana, whose sacred beast was the hare! Until about 1650 it was also customary to make finger rings from copper or brass coffin handles. If these were consecrated at the service of 'Creeping to the Cross' on Good Friday they would protect the wearer from cramp and fits!

Along the north wall of the chancel, many churches have an Easter Sepulchre. It was into this tomblike stone structure that the altar cross was removed on Good Friday evening. Two lighted candles, representing the two guardian angels flanked it. There it remained until the Vigil Mass on Sunday morning when, with the church in total darkness, the priest would light the Paschal candle with a new flame kindled in the early years by friction, but later by striking flint on steel. The congregation would light their lanthorns from the Passover Candle. After mass they would use the new flame to fire the hilltop beacons, lit to welcome the risen Lord while they waited for the dawn.

The bonfires were ancient symbols to purify the growing crops and were originally lit to honour 'Vesta' the Goddess of the sacred fire and of the hearth, whose flame must never be extinguished or disaster would strike - and from whom we get the brand name given to waxed matches!

The Venerable Bede wrote that Easter derives its name from Eostre, the Anglo-Saxon Goddess of the dawn and of Spring whose festival was held at the Equinox. The Council of Nicea decreed in 325 AD that Easter should be the Sunday after the Paschal full moon, following the vernal equinox (21st March). So it has to fall between 22nd March and 25th April, in what used to be called the Eostremonath (Easter month).

In Cheshire many people visited Rostherne Mere at dawn on Easter Sunday because a mermaid would ring the bell at the bottom of the lake, then sit on it and sing sweetly. From their mereside or hilltop vantage points, they would wait to watch the sun rise slowly above the horizon, for it was claimed that it danced for joy at the news of the resurrection. Afterwards the parishioners would wend their way home and if they weren't wearing something new the birds might well shed their droppings on them in disgrace! Back home their forty days of Lenten abstinence ended with a special meal that still bears its original meaning, BREAK-FAST, the main item on the menu being eggs, they were fried, scrambled, made into a sweet green herbal tansy omelet, soft boiled or hard boiled, dyed and decorated. Some of the latter would be saved for 'pace-egging' when they were rolled down the grassy slopes in remembrance of the stone being rolled away from the entrance to the tomb and of even older forgotten fertility rites.

Children found even more coloured eggs hidden around the house and garden. They had been 'laid' by the Easter Hare (the symbol of Diana the Moon Goddess). Christianity replaced the hare with the Easter bunny. Others explained that the church bells had travelled all the way to Rome to collect the eggs, which was why the bells hadn't been heard ringing on the 'still days' between Maundy Thursday and Easter Morning. But how did the egg become the symbol of Easter? A thousand years before the coming of Christ, the Chinese exchanged elegantly painted and decorated eggs during the Spring festival. The custom continued and spread throughout the Middle Eastern Empires of the Persians, Egyptians, Greeks and Romans. In many parts of Europe scarlet Easter Eggs were planted in fields and vineyards to protect the crops from storms and hail. In medieval England, landlords received a payment of eggs at Easter from their tenants.

Up to a century ago, beautifully patterned pace eggs, exhibited in tall ale-glasses, acted as a centrepiece on the sideboard to bring good luck and from early times broody hens were purposely put to start incubating their clutch of thirteen eggs (all marked with a cross) the day before Mothering Sunday - geese were started a week earlier. When the eggs were checked on Good Friday they were just eggs, but when you visited them on Easter morning they had hatched into cheeping little balls of living yellow fluff.

From Easter eggs to Easter chicks - a continuing life in a fresh form - a new beginning - a Resurrection!

36 May Hidden Energy
AGE-OLD PUZZLES SOLVED AT LAST - WHY DO COWS FORM A QUEUE?

For years it has puzzled me that when my cows have the free run of the fields they always seem to give birth to their calves on the self same spot, and when I bring them in for milking twice each day, they quite literally queue up to wait their turn to amble along towards the gate. They follow one another in single file, nose to tail on their narrow, well worn meandering cattle tracks, yet there is a whole wide open unused expanse on either side of them. Why are the older fields such queer shapes, when square or rectangular blocks would be so much more easy to manage? Or, a question that I have been asked by grown ups and children alike, is why do farmers always put gateways in the muddiest part of the field? And why do country lanes twist and turn like a snake in a contortionists' act, when everyone knows that the quickest way to get from A to B is in a straight line?

Well, I think that at last I've found the connecting link to these and many more questions. Though in discovering a possible solution I find that my new-found fund of knowledge poses even more problems than my original queries!

It all started to happen a few weeks ago, when a couple of local gravediggers were several feet down a grave in our churchyard. I went across and had a chat with them on my way to fetch my cows in for milking. They both posed the same question, considering it had been dry for so long, why was there so much water still flowing into the bottom of the grave? Not just in this churchyard, but in all the six where they had dug graves that week.

I started to think - I vaguely remembered reading that ancient mounds were usually built over powerful underground water currents. I delved deeper and discovered that the size and shape of the long, round or horned barrows, tumuli and cairns that were built four to seven thousand years ago were dictated by the strength of particular

patterns of energy that emerged from the earth beneath. About half these patterns were associated with moving water and blind springs that bubbled, burst and flowed under the surface in a similar way to springs that emerged into the light of day.

Churches were built on these ancient religious sites of barrows and tumuli. The central blind spring being marked inside our present day churches by a step and altar rail at the spot where the altar originally stood before it was placed against the east wall. If other blind springs were present these gave the position of the Lady Chapels, the font, stoups and steps, either up or down. If within the confines of the building there was a particularly important blind spring that threw out 'spirals' of energy, a 'spire' would be built above to indicate its position. The number of ornamental string courses built into the spire corresponded with the number of coils in the underground spiral cone of power.

Piscinas - small stone basins set into the wall of the church, usually on the south side, were always positioned over a water line. They carried the water away after the purification of the chalice. Where there is no Piscina the priest drinks this water after cleansing the vessel to prevent its profane use. Crypts and charnel houses (where exhumed bones were stored until being put on the bone-fire on October 31st) usually contain a maze of water lines that have a depressing effect, humbling penitents who were put therein to confess their sins.

Another line that is found in all churches built on these principles is the 'track line'. This, like the line that my cows follow consciously, we follow subconsciously. It must never be obstructed. This means that wherever a track line enters or leaves the building, there must be a door. Some churches only have one, others have many more than are needed and several of these have been blocked up by authorities who obviously did not realise the symbolic importance of their positional placing. The main footpaths that radiate from these doors follow those same track lines. The perimeter of the churchyard was defined by the nearest water line. If the water line was doubled the churchyard was raised a few feet because the barrow on which it was built was raised.

The porch was usually built over a blind spring as were lych gates and other entrances. If there were two tracks entering the churchyard, side by side, the stronger would be marked by the main gate and the lesser by a small wicket gate. In churches where this happened the men walked through the main gate but the women were only allowed through the wicket gate and, sometimes, they were also segregated inside the church as well.

Corpses were rested at 'weeping crosses', lych gates and in the porch en route. As these were all situated on blind springs, they gave extra energy to the soul of the deceased to ease its way to paradise - according to ancient theological thinking.

Because the church builders of olden times had to build in accordance with the patterns of invisible but essential energy which came from Mother Earth, they devised these codes of construction. To the outsider they are incomprehensible, but easily understood by those initiated into their secrets. Where possible, country cottages were also built over water spirals. This made the occupants happier and more contented - and may be why so many wish to live on these sites today!

The Bible has several references to the importance of these energy patterns that were well known to their rulers and priests. In Proverbs 8, Wisdom is said to be found over the blind springs, at the top of high places, at the doors and at the gates. The biblical name given to a blind spring was Bethel - where God dwells, it usually contained seven in-flowing spirals culminating at the centre of the altar.

But to come back to my introduction - to find out why my cows calve in the same place, I have since dowsed over that area with my divining rods and, sure enough, there is a blind spring underneath - they feel its influence. They also naturally follow the 'track line' on their way into milking - that also deflects my divining rods! Fields are such queer shapes because they were laid out initially by priests or dowsers. Where the water line surrounded an area a ditch was dug down to it and the hedge planted on top of the surplus earth. Where a natural geodetic force was encountered the hedge was raised on a bank - but there is no ditch.

Gates in fields, as in churchyards, are positioned over blind springs because they are said to act as signposts to animals. In wet weather the constant treading of the hooves and the blind spring beneath that hampers drainage, causes a morass - the muddiest part of the field! Our country lanes are crooked because they were once animal tracks that man has since overlaid with his roads.

And to my two friends bailing out the water from the grave, all I can say is that they will have to carry on bailing as I have discovered that there are many blind springs and underground rivulets in the churchyard - that was the reason for building the church on that particular site in the first place. It was the only place in the area where all the known patterns of energy combined to enable those who entered to worship, feel happier, more contented, and also gain in wisdom!

That's why churches last and people look after them - They are their *Bethel-*lehems! And, if you pass my farm and happen to see me leaning on the gate, I'm not foolishly idling my time away as you may at first think, no -

15 minutes later

.....it's my way of gaining wisdom!

37 June
JOYS - AND ACHES - OF OLD-STYLE HAYMAKING

Hanging on our living room wall is a picture that my son spotted in a local antique shop. It shows three women in Victorian working clothes, white blouses, long pleated skirts and white linen bonnets, who are tenderly turning swaths of hay with long handled rakes and forks. A younger lady, better dressed and with a straw hat is looking on. As well as depicting how hay harvesting was carried on at the turn of the century, an even stranger coincidence is that it was painted on our farm. That particular field is a narrow sloping slang, just south-east of the church, called the 'Mad Croft'. It has many humps and hollows, one of which was formerly a cockfighting pit! If those ladies could step out of the picture and into our present age they would probably agree that the principles of making hay haven't changed, only the means of achieving it.

For nowadays, we employ machinery instead of people! The grass has to be cut, dried by sun and wind, then gathered in as quickly as possible before the onset of rain.

The fastest that I had ever accomplished this feat, when all the conditions were perfect, was in two days! It usually takes five or six days and in inclement weather that can stretch to as many weeks.

Before the introduction of mechanical mowing machines in the 1850s, all hay fields had to be cut laboriously with scythes. On many farms this continued until the outbreak of the 1914-18 war. If the grass was in ear and the weather set fair for a few days, the regular gang of farmworkers, plus any outside help they could muster, would start to mow the outside swaths of the first field around about mid-day. They would continue scything until late evening and start again soon after dawn next morning, hoping to finish that field by noon. The reason for not cutting all the hay on the same day (as was the common practice with corn) was because the outside swaths of hay take longer to dry than the inner ones.

As soon as the dew had risen in the morning the ladies and older children would start to turn over the partially wilted outside rows of hay. They would gradually work their way round and round the field in ever decreasing circles until they finally turned what the men had cut that morning. Then back to the start, to do it all again, and again, and again.

Pastures were for grazing only, meadows were for mowing, and in bygone days flowers abounded, from the tiny time-telling scarlet pimpernel - the poor man's weatherglass - to bogs of speedwell, 'bird's-eye' blue, knots of golden buttercups and the white lace-like flowers of the cow and sheep's parsley. Overshadowing all, the swaying stems of the ox-daisy supported the tender tendrils of blue vetches which intermingled with crimson clover and yellow alsike - a riot of natural colour that is seldom seen in the fields of today.

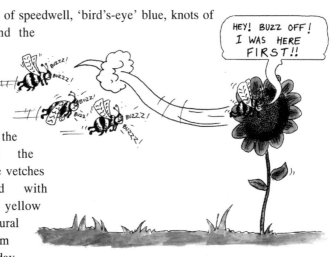

HEY! BUZZ OFF! I WAS HERE FIRST!!

Yet this peaceful country scene was a hive of activity; for the common flowers and herbs of the hay field also yielded a harvest of honey for the ever busy bees.

At haysel and harvest the farmer provided all his workers with an abundance of free drink, barrels of 'small' weak beer or cider according to the custom of the district, and on dairy farms buttermilk for the children. These, together with bottles of cold, unsweetened mint or raspberry leaf tea, were downed with relish to quench their thirst. After each round of mowing the men would stop for a short rest, sharpen their scythes, whet their whistles, then off they'd go again, laughing and joking, their scythes swinging rhythmically in muscular magnificence.

Each scythe was specially set according to its owner's stature and only he could comfortably use it. If the field was stony and hadn't been rolled, the grass stems were cut a bit higher to avoid blunting the blades. Molehills were another menace, for not only did the soil dull the edge but the earth would cling to the damp grass and if carried in on the hay, would contaminate it, make it gritty and unpalatable to the stock.

The highlights of each day were the 'bagins' - the meals. From the farmhouse would be carried large wicker baskets, covered with spotless white napkins and laden with rabbit pies, newly baked bread, hunks of cheese, scones and cakes. All the harvest team sat down and picnicked together, men and women, boys and girls, grandparents and grandchildren. Some sat on the half dried swaths, some sat on little haycocks, some sat on their jackets and some stretched out, relaxing in the warm sun.

Afterwards the younger and more energetic workers would play games with the children, burying them under piles of hay, chasing and catching them. There would be leap-frogging, hiding in the hedgerows or climbing trees to see who could reach the now empty nests. Then all too soon it was back to work.

Slowly the colour of the field changed from dark green to light green. With each tossing and turning the swaths became lighter and fluffier. All the time a close watch had to be kept on the sky, birds, flowers and animals, for the first signs of approaching rain or thunderstorms, for that determined how the crop was to be treated. If the hay was reasonably dry, but not sufficiently so to be carried into the buildings, when rain threatened it could be saved from a soaking by making it into haycocks or pikes. These were about five feet in diameter and about seven feet high - round stacks in miniature form. It was customary to make an extra large one for the children to play on and slide down first, then they wouldn't damage the rest, if they did their ears were boxed or their backsides tanned!

As each pike was completed, the outside was raked gently downwards so that the hay stems acted as a thatch and kept the rain out of the rest. Although the pikes would warm up and steam, especially in calm, damp weather, the hay inside was maturing and relatively safe from storms. They could remain outside for weeks without deteriorating, but they did have to be moved en-masse with horse and rope and dragged a few feet each week to prevent the grass being killed underneath them. When a suitable sunny and windy day arrived, the haycocks were opened and the hay spread around the area to dry further. Then all was carried into the barn or the cowshed and stable lofts ready for winter. It could then be fed directly into the mangers and feeding racks below with a minimum of further effort. Surplus hay was built into stacks outside and after being allowed to settle for at least a fortnight, they were thatched with straw to shed the rain.

Yes, life proceeded at a much more leisurely pace in those days and there were more hands to help with the work. Nowadays, my contractor cuts the grass at a speed undreamed of by the scythers of yesteryear. Then I bustle and bounce around the field on my noisy little tractor for three or four days, tedding, turning and rowing the crop. My contractor reappears with another machine that compresses the hay into bales which, with the help of a few hardworking friends, are carted home and stored in the barn.

Perhaps the main progress that we have made by employing machinery in place of people is that instead of several aching backs during the majority of the haymaking season there is now only one - and that's mine!

I wonder if the ladies in that picture would agree? For as they say - every picture tells a story!

38 July
'QUICK' HEDGES THAT TOOK FOURTEEN YEARS TO GROW

What is it that never moves, yet remains a constantly changing feature of our countryside? Its shape and colour differ with every season. And even though there are so many, no two are ever the same? It transforms what would otherwise be a monotonous and uninspiring landscape into a panoramic hotch-potch of picturesque patchwork parcels? Yes, by now you've probably guessed the answer: it is a HEDGE.

In stock farming areas hedges are still so plentiful that we tend to take them for granted as though they have always been there - but they haven't! A few lengths can trace their lineage back to the days of the Saxons. Many more originated around Tudor times from 1460 to 1600. But the majority were planted between 1740 and 1830, during the time of the Enclosures of the common land. A few have been added since. Generally they were sited to mark the position of a boundary, often with a drainage ditch dug alongside. The hedges were planted on the bank of spoil. They made a cheap division that all could see, when labour costs were low and the large amount of time taken to maintain them properly was of little importance. Indeed, some of the earliest hedges and ditches marked county boundaries, for the word 'shire' means 'marked out and cut off'.

But not all areas were climatically suitable to grow such a beautiful boundary. For example, where the land lay too high above sea level, where it was too windy or the soil too shallow for trees and hedges to grow, then our ancestors built walls instead. They utilised the stones and boulders cleared from the adjacent fields. On low, wet lands hedges wouldn't grow with their roots always standing in water, so ditches and dykes were dug. They had the dual purpose of aiding drainage, as well as forming the boundary. If the soil was infertile and unable to support a hedge, the boundary was simply a raised bank of turf or heather. When slightly more fertile these sod banks could support scrub or gorse on top.

Hedges do not necessarily have to be alive. When moving in hostile countryside, Roman soldiers carried sufficient 'pales' with them to erect a protective surrounding fence - a palisade - when resting or at night. They stayed 'within the pale', whilst their enemies whom they thought were outside the bounds of civilised behaviour, were 'beyond the pale'. These stake palisades or 'dead hedges' could also be interwoven with branches and be made into hurdles, six foot in length. Several hurdles fastened loosely together made a light-weight portable fence that could easily be folded up and moved to a new position; when used to contain stock it was called a fold! Some hurdles had their gaps filled with straw. These made windproof walls for lambing pens. Others were thatched with rushes to form the roof. Another use for hurdles was as a barrier in cross-country races!

In the medieval period, when three-field strip farming was practised, corn was protected by post and pollarded rail fencing. Scrub, brambles and thorns took root under them and gradually provided a permanent hedge against straying stock. Where woodland was cleared, the perimeter fence was made from transplanted saplings that would otherwise have been destroyed. This was called an assart hedge. By a law introduced during the reign of Richard I, it became an offence to allow it to grow above four feet six inches - the height that deer could jump when being chased for sport.

It wasn't until farmers moved from the centre of the villages onto the unfenced common land on the outskirts of the parishes, that the abundance of hedges, as we know them today, really came into being. During the hundred years following the 1740s, thousands of miles of field and farm boundaries were suddenly required. The best hedges were made of hawthorn, also called hedgethorn and quickthorn. It was not called 'quick' because of the speed with which it grew, but because it made a hedge that was alive (quick) as opposed to the pales and hurdles, which were dead.

Establishing a sturdy stockproof hedge was anything but quick; it was a long and time consuming business. First the hawthorn berries had to be mixed with sand and stored below ground in a rotting pit, for eighteen months. They were sown in soil in the spring, transplanted at two years old, and when four, planted in their permanent position, four inches apart, sixteen thousand to the mile, sufficient to enclose a farm of forty acres. They had to be weeded regularly and protected from animals for a further eight years. At about seven feet high they were cut and layered when there was no sap in the stems, making an interwoven 'quick' hedge - after fourteen years!

A hundred years ago Richard Jefferies wrote "The billhook is the national weapon of the English farmworker, most of the winter is spent hedging and layering."

But did you realise that it is possible to tell in which age a hedge was planted? Like many a country conundrum, it's easy when you know how. Count the number of different species along a thirty-three yard length of hedge, e.g. hawthorn, holly, elderberry, hazel, dogrose, sloe, etc., (not brambles). Usually every species along this stretch of lowland hedge represents one hundred years of establishment. Two species will date it as two hundred years old and probably planted during the Enclosures. Five species makes it a Tudor hedge. Ten different types and you are looking at something that existed before the Norman Conquest!

The first time I ever really consciously noticed the neatness of a well-kept hedge was one afternoon when I was cycling a different way home from school. A half-mile length of hawthorn that bordered each side of a narrow country lane had just been cut by hand. A co-ordination of mind and muscle, brain and brawn, that left it neater than any mechanical means could do it today. Not a leaf nor twig was out of place. The hedge was level and even as far as the eye could see. Trimmed with a pride that must have given that farmhand a deep sense of satisfaction, he was a country craftsman who obviously enjoyed his work. Little did I realise that one day I, too, would have similar lengths of hedge on view to passers-by. I often wonder if the way I try to maintain mine will ever inspire anyone else? But at least I do know that although most of my farm hedges are only a hundred years old, I've got one that was probably planted in Tudor times and a little way away, I think I've spotted a Saxon one!

Our ancestors certainly knew the advantages of having a living hedge as a boundary, for an ancient proverb advises - 'A hedge between keeps friendship green', whilst another adds - 'Love your neighbour, but don't rip up your hedges'!

39 August
FREE BEER HELPED TO BRING THE HARVEST HOME

HARVEST COSTREL

Blustery breezes blow over the fields of ripening corn. Their movement creates a contrast of sunshine and shadows which look like waves rolling across the sea. Flocks of sparrows sweep in from the shelter of the surrounding hedgerows to raid the headland corn. Free food for all and plenty to spare. Pigeons, rooks and geese are more wasteful, for as they land their weight flattens an increasingly large area of corn and they constantly tread down more and more. They take little notice of the regular firing of the automatic acetylene banger. And even less of the motionless scarecrow that has stood rooted to the same spot for several days, with a dead rook swinging open-winged on a string beneath each extended arm.

Fortunately for the farmer, not all the grain matures at the same time. By careful planning, a continuity of ripening can be achieved, usually in the order of winter sown barley, winter wheat, spring barley, spring wheat but also according to variety and soil conditions. During these past hot days, many of the winter sown crops have been harvested by the combine. It gorges the hardened grain that has ripened on its standing stalk, strips away the protective chaff covering and disgorges the chaff and straw in a continuous cloud of dust from its rear. Within a day the colour of the field is changed from gleaming gold to morbid black as the stubbles are burned.

How different from the slower change of scene before the arrival of machines, when the shortest possible time from cutting to clearance was, by tradition, seventeen days! It was during July in those days that farmworkers would appoint their fastest and best worker as 'Lord of the Harvest', the second fastest was the 'Lady of the Harvest'. These two men would agree a contract price with the farmer for the gathering in of the whole of his corn crops. From then on the harvest became the workmen's responsibility. The farmer was duty bound to provide free beer, cider and buttermilk during this period and at the conclusion a slap up meal for all who had helped.

When the first field had turned from green to gold the gang of workers would gather at dawn along the headland, scythes sharpened to a razor-edge. The fastest worker, 'The Lord of the Harvest' would set into the corn and start mowing a swath about a yard wide. The cut corn was collected in a hazelwood cradle at the bottom of the scythe handle and left in a neat pile at the end of each sweep. These made up into a continuous row as he edged forward foot by foot. When he had gone a yard or two the 'Lady of the Harvest' followed, scything a yard deeper into the field. Then the third man, and so on up to the last, usually the eighth man. Together they mowed a strip eight yards wide around the field. Each kept a respectable distance from the next to avoid getting his legs scythed, which is why the fastest always went first.

They purposely worked in teams, not only for companionship, but also to get the field done in a day. Each man could cut about an acre a day, so eight men could mow eight acres, most fields were about that size and it gave them an added incentive to keep at it. There was also the additional excitement of chasing and catching rabbits. When only a small patch of standing corn remained the whole team, their wives and families, would stop work, pick up their sticks and stalk the rabbits, hitting them senseless. Some men were very accurate with 'throwing sticks' or stones. Others would mark the burrows into which escaping rabbits had scuttled. These would be dug out for sport in the evening. The reward of rabbits was one of the few perks the farmworker had. If sold they were a welcome addition to his wages or, if eaten, a welcome nourishment for his often large and growing family.

The main task given to ladies and children at harvest was to tie the wheat and oats into bundles called sheaves, but barley, being too short to tie, was left in rows and carried loose, like hay. A stack of unthreshed barley destined for brewing was called a 'Mow', hence the pub name 'The Barley Mow'.

To form the band (bant, bont) which secured the wheat or oats into a sheaf, half a dozen corn stalks were held in each hand. The ears were tied together, the stalks were wrapped around the middle of the bundle, the overlapping thick ends were twisted up tightly and folded under the band to prevent them unravelling. Taking a sheaf under each arm, they were stood in neat rows, ears uppermost angled in the form of the letter A. Further pairs of sheaves were added on each side of the original two. These collectively were called stooks or kivvers. Children had great fun chasing around them, jumping over them, knocking them down, getting cussed and having to rebuild them. They were excellent for playing 'hide and seek' and provided a cool shelter from the heat of the sun. Sometimes a child, exhausted by his activities and tired of waiting to be found, would fall asleep and be 'missing' when the field was finished. Then the 'seeking' began in earnest and the 'hiding' often followed!

By tradition, cut corn and sheaves had to remain in the field until the church bells had rung over them three times before they were considered sufficiently mature and free from sap to be carried home. Some workers craftily cut their fields on a Saturday so that the sheaves would be vulnerable to the weather for the shortest possible time. For if a prolonged spell of rain set in, the sheaves would have to be turned inside out with thumbs and fingers - a real wrist-aching job. I know because I've had to do it many a time. The stooks would also have to be moved onto fresh ground regularly to avoid killing the grass growing beneath. An even worse hazard was warm, wet weather, when the grain would germinate and sprout in the stooks and be as green on top as the grass beneath. Then often half or more of the sheaves would have to be pulled away -

a depressing job as the growing grain was useless and the remainder was often mouldy or mildewy.

On the day the corn was due to be carted home to the farm, the sheaves were laid with their thick bottom butt ends facing the wind or sun to dry out. Every available cart, tumbril and wagon was pressed into service. Each had its own extension harvest ladders (gawmers, thrippers or riplings) to enable it to carry a larger load of the lightweight sheaves. Sheaves, loose corn and hay were all loaded in the same way, the outside layers first, inside last, row upon row upwards, then finally roped for the bumpy journey home. An extra horse was put in front to help pull the heavy load. This was called the 'trace' or 'cock'-horse.

At the farm the sheaves were unloaded inside the barn or outside in stacks. When all was finished the men were paid, they bought new boots and clothes for themselves and their families and the farmer provided the meal he had promised for bringing the 'Harvest Home'. Eating, drinking, dancing, singing and merrymaking often lasted all night and well into the following day. Our ancestors knew from experience that a bumper crop at the beginning of the harvest could change from fortune into famine by the end of the harvest if a prolonged wet spell set in. It's no wonder they celebrated in style when at last all was safely gathered in.

Today with our surpluses we do not have to worry unduly about where our next meal will come from, nor when it will be. So shouldn't we be a little more thankful that we have enough, and some to spare, when our harvest comes home?

40 September Drovers
WHEN CATTLE HERDS HOOFED IT HUNDREDS OF MILES TO MARKET - and dogs found their way back home on their own

When a cow calves she produces milk for about ten months, after an initial peak her production slowly subsides, she 'dries off' and has about two months rest from milking. Then another calf is born, more milk is given and the cycle continues. To remain profitable each of my cows has to produce a calf every year. Those that fail to do so are sent to market. It was the lorry calling to collect two of my barren cows that started me thinking of the changes that have occurred in moving animals to their destination. Nowadays all I have to do is pick up the phone and record my message on an answering machine. This is duly noted by the haulier who, hopefully, rolls up at the right farm on the right day for the animals who have an easy ride to market.

No longer do they have to hoof it as they did in days gone by. Cattle from Scotland and Wales were walked to the rich grazing grounds of the Midlands, East Anglia and around the metropolis where they feasted and fattened for a year and doubled in weight. Then they made their final journey to London in droves of up to a thousand strong. They halted all other traffic on the wide 'green' roads as they passed, much to the annoyance of other travellers. Before the railway system took over their transportation, two hundred thousand cattle and one and a half million sheep were walked into London every year to feed the population. It's no wonder that people complained about the stinking state of the 'high'-ways!

During the reign of Queen Elizabeth droving was an honourable occupation. To enter the profession you had to be thirty years old, married and vouched for annually by three J.P.s and even if you lost everything, bankruptcy was not allowed. Although a few rogues slipped through the net, the early drovers were mainly well educated, dedicated men who enjoyed dealing, travelling and caring for the stock in their charge, which were usually black and small.

At five years old most store cattle from Scotland, Ireland and Wales weighed only five hundred weight because of the inferior pastures. They were worth about five pounds each when sold to the drover at the farm gate, market or fair. They walked an average of two m.p.h. for seven to twelve hours a day, covering a hundred miles in a six day week. Sunday was an enforced day of rest and all toll charges were doubled on the Sabbath! Inns were frequent along the drove trails and driftways, many still bear the name 'Drovers Arms'. Nearby were small 'halfpenny' fields where cattle were rested and grazed at a ha'penny an animal a night. The drover and his dogs were fed and bedded for fourpence, but thrifty Scottish drovers preferred to sleep in the field with their animals and lived on a sparse diet of oatmeal and onions, whisky and water.

Drovers added to their income by delivering letters, family messages and important documents en-route and also carried tax money for the Crown. Extra hands were often provided by youngsters on their way to London to seek a fortune, become apprentices, articled clerks or work in the hop fields of Kent. On their return, drovers brought eagerly awaited news of victories, and of relatives and the details of the latest fashions. They were also industrious folk and often knitted knee-length stockings as they journeyed. Some were sold to people as they passed and some they wore themselves.

The feet and soles of their own stockings were always soaped before wearing, so that the sock would slide easily between the foot and the boot or clog and therefore not chaffe the skin and cause blisters! Soap and animal fats were also used to waterproof their garments, especially leggings as there were no wellingtons in those days. Lameness was a constant problem with the cattle. Wet and swampy pastures in the countries of origin made hooves soft and mis-shapen. They wouldn't stand up to a prolonged period of travelling across rugged terrain and stony tracks. To remedy this trouble the outside half of their cleft hooves were cold shoed with iron plates called 'cues' fastened on with three or five broadheaded nails, first dipped in pork fat to help heal any wounds caused!

A brawny blacksmith and his hefty helper could rope, throw, tie up, pare and shoe seventy animals a day at two pence a shoe - eight pence per beast. Should an animal cast its shoe or go lame on the journey, the head drover - the 'Topsman' - acted as blacksmith. He always carried spare supplies of nails and shoes - smeared with fat to stop them rusting. Any stock dying of disease on the journey had to be inspected and killed by the churchwarden of the village through which they were passing. Failure to do so carried an automatic fine of ten pounds. Cattle plague and rinderpest were notifiable diseases for which the Government paid compensation of half the market value of the slaughtered animal. The hide was slashed before burial to prevent anyone later removing the skin and selling it to the tannery for making into leather, possibly spreading the disease. Slashing also stopped the internal gases blowing the decomposing carcass up like a balloon and bursting out of the grave.

The approach of a drove herd was heralded by the blowing of horns and the constant calling of "Ho-ho, Ho-ho". This encouraged the loitering cattle forward and also gave farmers ahead time to confine their own stock - which might otherwise join the drove.

Dogs were an essential part of the system. The sturdy, trustworthy English cattle dog was the black and white 'cur', now known mainly as a sheepdog. The Welsh used Corgis that would nip at the heels of the cattle and, being so short legged, the resultant kick would pass over their heads. The Scots preferred the big brown and white long haired 'Collie' named after a now extinct breed of sheep. All were highly intelligent, resourceful and home loving - as well illustrated in the tear-jerking film 'Lassie Come Home'. Indeed, this frequently happened, because at the fair or market at the end of the 'stance', the drover collected his money for the cattle, paid his hired helpers and returned home, guarding his golden guineas by a slightly safer method - stage coach. The dogs were set free to find their own way back. They fed at their regular stopping places. The inn-keepers were paid at the next passing of the six to eight droves of the season. So strong was their homing instincts that the dogs often arrived a day or two ahead of their masters!

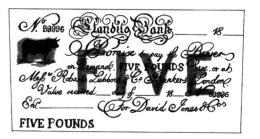

FIVE POUNDS

Carrying so much money, even by coach, was a hazardous business. Hold-ups by highwaymen, footpads, fellow travellers or dishonest innkeepers were thwarted when 'Bills of Exchange' were carried instead. These could only be cashed by bona-fide customers. It was in this way that in 1799, the Bank of the Black Ox, was founded in Wales (taken over by Lloyd's Bank in 1909).

It is certainly true that the 'Roast Beef of Old England' has helped to keep many an Irish, Welsh and Scottish farmer and stock-breeder solvent. And still the cattle come! From green-ways to railways and today on motorways, they are transported in cattle wagons across the length and breadth of England to be fattened on traditional pastures. Then they are conveyed to the abattoir, their joints like those of my barren cows, cut into suitable sizes to stock the shelves of the supermarkets in the cities. Nothing has really changed much over the years, only the methods of achieving it.

41 October
ERA PASSES AS SCRAPMEN MOVE INTO THE OLD MILL
THE DAY THE BLAST EXPERTS LIFTED THE ROOF

According to the date inscribed on one of the beams, for nearly three centuries our village mill has vibrated to the trundling of its four sets of millstones. It has reverberated to the slap of the flat driving belts as their spliced connections passed over the blacksmith-made pulleys on their long iron shafts, and echoed to the constant clacking of the 'damsels' that jogged the corn from the bottom of the hoppers to the chutes that led to the centres of the rotating mill stones.

For the first two hundred and twenty years, add to that the background noise of the rushing stream which constantly flowed onto the thirty-four foot diameter backshot water wheel - with all its attendant moans and groans. Then about fifty years ago the wheel was replaced by a diesel engine which has since 'put-put-putted' its noise and fumes into the atmosphere. There in sight and sound you have the scene that surrounded the six or seven men who worked there, and that greeted the parishioners who brought their grist to be ground at the mill.

Although the church provided the spiritual food of the parish, it was from the mill that they obtained their daily bread. For, in addition to its grinding facilities, the mill had a bake oven for the use of the estate and the parish. It also contained a drying kiln to reduce the moisture content of the corn. Its special two-inch thick clay brick floor was pin-pricked with eight one-eighth inch diameter holes, covering every square inch, to allow the heat to rise but not allow the grain to fall through. It was the job of the junior mill hand periodically to push a piece of wire through every one of those twenty-six thousand holes to make sure they were not clogged with dust and dirt. After completing that task he must have suffered from spots before his eyes!

To gain a sufficient head of water, a fifteen foot high semi-circular dam was built four hundred yards upstream adjoining the bridge by the site of the former undershot mill. This flooded about twenty acres of land, and created a locally famous wildfowl pool. Surplus water overflowed the dam wall and continued on its normal meandering journey down-stream. But the water required to drive the mill flowed along a culvert, first passing an iron sluice, screened by gratings, which held back most of the branches, reeds, and leaves that might otherwise have blocked the channel or damaged the wheel. The four foot brick lined culvert was originally open for most of its length and flowed close beside the inn door (now my farmhouse). I often wonder how many revellers fell in on their way home after their evening of indulgences. The water then forded the minor road and gathered in an open reservoir with stone walled sides and puddled clay underneath. At the mill end another iron grating protected a second sluice that fed a controlled amount of water underneath

what is now the A34 road, to turn the water-wheel, which at full bore developed forty horse-power.

If there was not enough water coming through, it may have been due to local lads playing pranks - they had wound down the screw and closed the sluice. Alternatively, rubbish was blocking the grating. If so, the debris was fished out with a long handled four tine fork with bent prongs called a krome. A much more serious problem was the silting up of the mill pond Many older villagers vividly remember the sight, smell and sound of the two large steam engines, one on each bank side, winching a two-way cable dredging bucket back and to, across the pool, leaving mounds of muddy spoil and reed roots on the bank behind them as they moved slowly along.

Our mill worked on the same principle as most others. The grain was stored on the top storey, emptied into hoppers that fed the stones on the second floor, the milled meal was bagged off on the bottom floor and sold or returned to another machine for further processing. The constant moving of corn on iron wheeled sack trucks had worn the wooden floors unevenly into grooves and hollows dotted with knotty projections. A chain hoist worked by the pull of a rope lifted the heavy hessian sacks through clattering half-hatch, elm doors. Their centre holes were worn into irregular patterns by the chafing of the loaded chain.

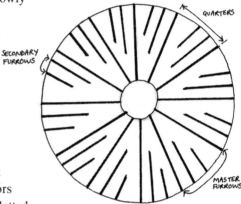

The hardest stones for grinding flour were imported French 'Burr'. Each millstone was made from a jigsaw like pattern of four central blocks and sixteen outer pieces, bedded in plaster of Paris and held in place by a thick outer iron band. They had sixteen grooves, known as furrows, at the centre, radiating through the chest to forty at the rim - the skirt. These furrows were generally cut anticlockwise (widdershins) on burr stones, but clockwise on Derbyshire millstone grit stones, hewn in one piece from the solid rock. They were slightly softer and used more for grinding animal feeds. The lower 'bed' stone remained stationary, the upper 'runner' stone revolved, creating a scissor cutting action on the grain, which was fed into the centre eye - kibbled in the eye furrows - cracked in the chest - and finished as flour at the skirt. The clearance between the stones was adjustable to suit the coarseness required.

Stones wore smooth and needed attention after about three hundred hours of grinding. The grooves were re-cut by a stone-dresser, using a mill-bill and thrift, rather like a small three pound pick. To protect his eyes from flying chips he squinted or wore

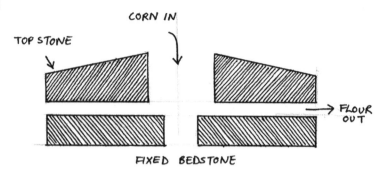

CORN IN

TOP STONE

FLOUR OUT

FIXED BEDSTONE

wire mesh protectors. An even earlier eye protection was made from the two halves of a walnut shell with a tiny hole bored in the centres! When after many, many years the eight inch thick stones were worn and dressed to three inches thick they were no longer stable and were discarded. Their final use was often as ornamental steps to decorate the miller's house or garden - as in mine. Replacement stones stood ready by the wall of the mill, while the deep window ledges inside held stocks of thin canvas and leather for splicing belts and spare pear-wood teeth - since the large iron toothed gear wheel engaged wooden toothed cogs to reduce noise, wear and friction.

A few years ago the estate sold some of the surplus mill machinery for scrap. One large flywheel defied all attempts to dismantle it. In desperation the scrapmen detonated a charge of dynamite beneath it to blow it to smithereens. But they miscalculated the amount and blew a large part of the mill roof off as well! I was told later that it had cost more to replace the roof than the scrap was worth!

From early Victorian times, demands upon the miller have gradually changed. The advent of the steam engine meant that many large farms found it more economical to grind their own cattle, pig and poultry corn. The miller had to rely on smaller farms and smaller orders. Steam ships replaced sailing ships, massive quantities of grain could be off-loaded at our ports cheaper than farmers could grow it. New mills were built at the dockside. The country corn miller became a corn merchant - becoming a small cog in their large sales machine - and his mill became a warehouse for other people's products. Now the majority of our small farms and smallholdings have also disappeared - swallowed up in the race to produce bigger units to reduce costs, and bigger farmers buy their corn in bulk, not bags, so the millstones stand idle.

The increasing overheads of rent, rates and maintenance, set against the reduced turnover, means that as a modern business, the small country corn mill is no longer viable. So at eighty our 'Dusty' miller has decided to call it a day and retire. Almost the only reminder of a lifetime spent grinding away for the community comes from his continual contact with corn dust - for he carries with him an unwrinkled complexion that would be the envy of many a cosmetic fashion model a quarter of his age!

Now the scrapmen have moved in, they are dismantling the remaining items of value but they are having a job with the cumbersome old diesel engine. One of them was considering putting a charge of dynamite underneath! I wonder if they will blow the roof off again?!!

42 November
HOW THE SCHOOL BELL CAME HOME TO ROOST

Our village school once stood somewhere in my garden. The pupils were said to learn to write by copying the letters carved on the gravestones in the adjacent churchyard. In 1721 a local nobleman donated a bell that was rung to summon the students to school and mark the periods of their lessons. The school was later moved to the quaint thatched cottages that still stand beside the main road. There twelve pupils at a time received an elementary education. In 1842 the school moved yet again, this time to a new and much bigger building opposite. On the roof was a turret, which housed the school bell.

About fifty years ago the rain started leaking into the headmaster's top storey flat, so the turret was dismantled and the bell stored in the outhouses at the vicarage. When these were recently cleared the long-forgotten bell came to light. The church council, in their wisdom, decided to install it beside the existing one in our church bell tower. Little did they realise that the bell was simply coming home to roost, for when the carpenter came to fix it in place, he found that all the holes required were already in the correct positions to receive it - including the one for the bell rope - the belfry was its original home! So, nowadays, before our church services we have two bells calling our parishioners to prayer - but that doesn't mean that we get twice as many in the congregation!

Over the past thousand years bells have played an important part in organising our day into its present divisions of hours and minutes. As each civilisation advanced, it apportioned the length of daylight into periods. The Saxons divided theirs into four 'tides', each corresponding to about three hours. The Romans had twelve 'hours' that varied in length according to the season - shorter hours in winter and longer in summer. But divisions of time weren't important in the countryside. People were awakened by the natural noises of birds and animals at dawn, they worked during the day and rested when darkness fell.

It was the religious institutions, the monks and nuns, who needed the correct time for their services. Accuracy was achieved by burning calibrated candles or by water dripping to fill small containers. The big breakthrough came in 996 A.D., when Gerbert, a Benedictine Monk, constructed a mechanical bell (clock) with weights as the motive power and a pendulum for control. He later became Pope - Sylvester II. Clocks developed steadily in religious houses and at controllable intervals a bell was struck - with an animated figure known as a 'jack' - to call everyone to prayer.

In England a clock-keeper was employed at St. Paul's in 1286 but no record exists of the mechanism. Westminster Abbey had a clock in 1290 and Canterbury Cathedral paid thirty pounds for one a couple of years later. Belfries were ideal vantage points for installing clocks, as they already had bells that could be utilised

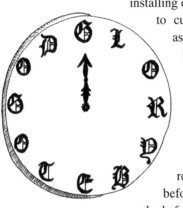

to cut the costs. A blacksmith's son erected the first astronomical clock at St. Albans in 1326 and later became its Abbot! The oldest still in existence were built around 1400 A.D. - one in Salisbury Cathedral, another nearby at Ottery St.Mary. Three more, erected by a Glastonbury monk, were at Exeter, Wells and Wimborne. Dials and a revolving hour hand were not introduced to the general public until the 1600s because so few people were capable of reading them; a further hundred years had to pass before the idea of a minute hand became accepted! Some clock faces bore letters instead of numerals, conveying the message 'Watch and Pray' or 'Glory be to God'.

But rural life carried on in the way it always had, these new-fangled notions and motions were all right for towns and cities - the country parson still preferred his sundial, scratched on the south wall of the church.

It consisted of a few lines radiating from a central hole, into which a pointed peg - a 'gnomon' - was placed. When the shadow from its point fell on a certain line it was time for the mass to begin. These simple timekeepers were called scratch dials or mass dials. But supposing the sun didn't shine, you ask? Well, they simply guessed as best they could and, since the service usually lasted three hours or

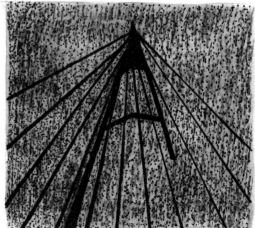

more, a few minutes mistake either way wouldn't have made much difference!

Inside the church and immediately beside the pulpit stood another means of measuring time - the hour glass. Fine sand ran through a narrow neck from a glass container above into another below and indicated the expected length of the parson's sermon, anything shorter and the preacher was considered lazy! Local records state that in 1623 Prestbury parish paid 'fifteen pence for an hour glass and twenty pence for a 'sett' (frame) for same' - it was later gilded. Whilst at Wilmslow they seemed to suffer badly from breakages, as they required replacements or repairs in 1635, 1645 and 1655!

But, coming back to clocks, the improvement produced by a spring instead of weights and an escapement to replace the pendulum reduced the size of clocks and allowed the production of pocket watches. These became fashionable and were worn as status symbols by all who could afford them. In 1797 William Pitt tried to raise revenue by taxing watches and clocks. Poorer people were forced to part with their prized possessions. To compensate, inns and post taverns erected special time pieces for the benefit of their customers. These are now referred to as 'Act of Parliament' clocks. Liquor could be freely obtained on short credit and paid for later, known colloquially both then and now, as 'on tick'. In establishments where no credit was given a clockface was sometimes painted on the wall to denote 'no tick'.

Clocks were set by the maximum elevation (Zenith) of the sun, at mid-day. This varied by several minutes between our East and West coasts; there was no standard time. Every area had its own local time, which caused considerable confusion. Exactly one hundred years ago, in 1884, a conference at Washington decided to make Greenwich the mean-time and adjust all others to it, so that in future no one need be unduly inconvenienced or arrive late because of variations of time.

Even so, it frequently happens when I'm due to take the service in my local church that, in spite of having nearly twenty clocks and watches in my farmhouse - and nowadays having TWO bells to call me to prayer - I am generally still the last person to pass through the church door before the service begins!

P.S. The rumours that my congregations are looking out for a ten minute 'hour' glass are totally unfounded!

43 WANDERING WOOLLIES
or The Tale of the Lost Sheep

*This is an extra little story so that I could fill this little book completely
for you - and also give a good even number to finish on.*

The evidence was unmistakable, they'd visited me again. There, hanging from the barbs
of the boundary fence, were tell-tale wisps of white wool. My next door neighbour's
sheep had paid me yet another visit - or so I thought. Little did I realise at the time that
I might be wrong.

Many years ago, when he first moved next door with his two young sons, he had
cleared all the boundary hedges and fences. Rusty wire, broken posts and dead branches
were all removed and new posts put in where required. Rolls and rolls of strong, squared
sheep netting were stapled to the posts, together with two strands of barbed wire at six
inch intervals which combined to make his boundary fences the most stockproof in the
area. Neither sheep, cow, pony nor horse dared venture to the greener grass that always
grew on the other side (my side!). Over the years he has been an excellent neighbour -
the only time we ever seem to meet is at church or village functions, or distantly when
fetching our respective herds in for milking.

Then about five years ago it started happening. The sheep netting, once shiny,
bright and galvanised, was starting to rust; the first few joints were beginning to part.
With a bit of extra effort the smallest lambs
discovered they could squeeze through the
elongated holes. It wasn't long before
the ewes found that by exerting a
bit more pressure they could
enlarge the holes sufficiently to
join their young. Once one or
two found they could get
through, the whole flock soon
followed - just like a lot of sheep!
Usually their errant ways were
quickly discovered. With a few well-
directed whistles from my neighbour, they

were soon rounded up with the help of his black and white
sheepdog. Back on the right side of the fence the hole was patched with any handy piece
of wire, often from the pile of old hay baling wire.

This had one distinct disadvantage - not being galvanised, it soon rusted and
things rapidly went "haywire" again; or else the sheep just made a fresh hole
somewhere else. One corn harvest they came through and stayed for two or three days
before he had time to leave his combining and fix the fence. I didn't worry; sheep

possess "golden hooves". They enrich the pasture with their droppings which helps to compensate for the grass they eat.

My neighbour was most apologetic. "I'll make it right" he said, and true enough a few days later he called with half a dozen lovely tender lamb chops - the kind that almost melt in your mouth - they were delicious, taken from one of the lambs which had formerly been a trespasser but was now filling his deep freeze. Those chops were so nice that I rather felt like opening up a few more holes to let them through again, then I might get another tasty dinner from him!

So the other week, when I saw those fresh wisps of wool on the boundary fence, I felt sure I might be well on the way for some more chops. The sheep were grazing away contentedly and my mouth was watering everytime I looked at them. Coming out of church after service the next Sunday I casually remarked to him that his sheep seemed to be enjoying themselves on my field. "My sheep?" he exclaimed. "I sold the rest of mine about a month ago". My heart sank - no more lamb chops. "Oh no", he said, breaking into my thoughts, "They'll belong to old Fred." (quite a few farms further away). "They're always getting out".

They were, as I discovered next morning when the 'phone rang. "I hear you've get some of my sheep grazing on your fields," says Fred. "I've been searching high and low for them for the last few days. You send them back right sharpish," he says irately, slamming the 'phone down. My vision of more appetising lamb chops melted completely away.

I soon sent the ewes scuttling back onto my neighbour's land and he likewise onto his neighbours. When last I heard of them they were off again, going in the opposite direction.

As the nursery rhyme says, "Leave them alone and they'll come home, wagging their tails behind them".

Or, as old Fred once sarcastically stated when I remarked on his nomadic flock looking so content and 'wagging their tails behind them,' "Well, you'd hardly expect 'em to wag 'em in front, would you?"

44 December

BEEFEATERS, BLACKGUARDS AND ALL THAT CODSWALLOP
Words & Sayings and Their Origin

Have you ever wondered how certain words and sayings started - especially if they have changed their meaning over the years. Have you been amazed when you realised the close connection between phrases that are used so frequently that you've never stopped to think about them - until their origin was pointed out? I find it a fascinating subject. Here are a few of my favourites.

In olden days servants were termed 'eaters', and were divided into two classes. The lower the status, the more dishonest they were assumed to be. At meal times, those

in positions of authority sat 'above the salt' with their master and because they were allowed to eat meat, they were called 'beef-eaters'. Servants who were not so highly favoured sat 'below the salt' and, as their diet consisted largely of bread, they were called 'loaf-eaters' or 'loafers'. At the bottom end of the scale were the rowdy and often unruly kitchen staff. Because they were constantly engrained with grease and grime from the fire-blackened cooking appliances, and when travelling had to guard the kitchen utensils against theft or damage, they were called 'blackguards' - 'blaggards'. A very close watch was always kept on them and their thieving antics, sometimes by an independent medieval mercenary on the lookout for the best paid job, a 'free-lance'.

Pious pilgrims rode to Canterbury at a leisurely pace to visit the tomb of Thomas a Becket. Their ambling gait was called the 'Canterbury gallop', but this expression has since been reduced to a 'canter'. At night they rested in 'hospitality houses' provided by the religious orders, some of which evolved into our 'hostels' and 'hotels'. Their horses were housed under the scrutiny of the 'hostelier' - 'ostler', who was the local 'Master of the Horse' and 'Count of the Stable'. He was responsible for maintaining law and order in the Hostelry. Later his arm became lengthened, but his name became shortened to 'Con-stable'.

Pilgrims and other unfortunate travellers caught in a storm might be able to shelter under the overhanging eaves of a thatched cottage. Being so close to the wall and next to the window they would be able to overhear any comments made inside, and so 'eavesdrop' on the conversation.

Every village contained its characters. Their ridicule was accepted as a part of parish life. A person with wealth and whimsical ideas was said to have a maggot in his brain and was often nicknamed 'Maggoty' (Johnson at Gawsworth). It was also the name given to a fanciful dance. Other explanations of odd behaviour were richly illustrated both in words and imagination by incidents taken from nature around them, such as 'bees in the bonnet' and 'bats in the belfry'. Meanwhile the village idiot wandered harmlessly around 'wool gathering'. In our modern society this once common occupation has died out. The mentally deficient are no longer able to roam freely and, as a result, the phrase has lost most of its meaning. For today we do not scour the hedgerows, bushes, brambles and thorns, gathering tufts of sheep's wool for weaving - a little bit here and a little bit there, wherever it has become entangled. To a distant observer those meanderings were without rhyme or reason - they were just woolly-headed wool gatherers!

When imbeciles had to be taken into the 'workhouse', the only job many were capable of learning was to turn the crank handle, hence the term 'cranky'. Able bodied men entering were given a heavy hammer, a large pile of stones and told to 'get cracking', reducing the rocks to a suitable size to mend the potholes in the road. Those who were too feeble, frail or too ill to enter the workhouses were admitted into 'hospitality' houses that have now become the 'hospitals' and 'hospices' of our land.

Visiting the village regularly was a tinker. He sold pots and pans and mended worn ones. To make sure that the solder did not escape through the hole, he made a 'cuss' of clay or rolled a small pellet of moistened bread which he stuck to the underside of the hole to act as a dam. The repair completed, the now useless cuss was thrown away - but arrived in our lap as the expression 'not worth a tinker's cuss'. Another caller was the 'cadger' - or 'badger', as he was called in many parts of Cheshire, after the name of the basket he carried. He was an itinerant dealer, haggler and carrier of butter, eggs and country produce. He bought items as cheaply as possible from the farms and sold them as expensively as possible in the nearby towns. His unscrupulous trading soon brought his name into disrepute. 'Gypsies' also hawked their wares. They were so called because they were thought to have come from Egypt - a corruption of Egyptians!

Shepherds wiled away their long hours of boredom by using a long knife called a 'whittle' to cut small pieces from sticks and horns. So they 'whittled' away at their sticks and 'whittled' away their time.

Although we measure our time mainly in days, did you realise we occasionally

measure it in nights? A 'fortnight' is simply an abbreviation of fourteen nights and a week was once called a se'en night.

It is not only bellringers who 'drop a clanger' - when the bell rings out of turn. Cornish miners did it in another way. Their wives baked a complete meal within a Cornish pasty. It had meat in one half and jam in the other. To 'drop a clanger' mixed the two ingredients together into a terrible mess! Whilst working you might be told to 'whet your whistle', which was really a musical term which meant to sharpen it because your tune was flat, so you had a drink. If the beer had been stored at too high a temperature it went fizzy and was called 'wallop'. About 1870 Hiram Codd invented a bottle sealed by gaseous pressure against a glass marble in the neck, that could contain an effervescent lemonade. It was dubbed 'Coddswallop' and, as the lemonade didn't taste a bit like fizzy beer, the word soon became to mean 'a nonsense'. Which is rather like the fact that when omnibuses were introduced, they were pulled by horses. Some drivers became so attached to their animals, that on their day off they would ride as a passenger on their own bus to make sure that their horses were not being ill-treated - hence 'a busman's holiday'.

And, speaking of horses, do you remember when you were a teenager, making yards and yards of 'french knitting' on four pins around a hollow dolly, also known as a 'knitting Nancy', then using the result as reins to keep young children under control? Well, I was once told - though I've never read it anywhere - that when used as reins they were called ta-ta's and that is why when children go out with their reins on, they are going 'ta-ta's.

So ta-ta for now and, if you have enjoyed reading these articles as much as I have enjoyed writing them, then it has certainly all been well worth while. I'm off to compile my next book.

the end.